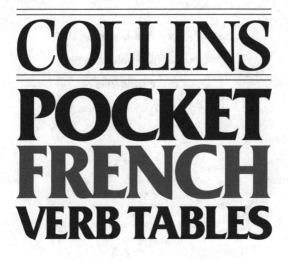

COLLINS
POCKET
FRENCH
VERB TABLES

HarperColli

First published in this edition 1993

© HarperCollins Publishers 1993

Latest reprint 1996

ISBN 0 00 472026-1 Paperback

Lesley A Robertson

editorial staff
Megan Maxwell

editorial management
Vivian Marr

series editor
Lorna Sinclair Knight

---

*A catalogue record for this book
is available from the British Library*

*Typeset by Tradespools Ltd, Frome, Somerset
Printed and bound in Great Britain
by Caledonian International Book
Manufacturing Ltd, Glasgow, G64*

INTRODUCTION

Your **Collins Pocket French Verb Tables** is a handy quick-reference
guide to one of the most important aspects of the French language. All
the essential information about French verbs and how to use them is
covered and the innovative use of colour throughout the text makes
learning verb endings and irregularities easy – and fast!

The book is divided into three sections. The first section gives a
detailed explanation of each of the three French verb conjugations,
showing the regular endings in each conjugation for all the main tenses,
along with instructions on how to form the present participle, the past
participle and the imperative in each conjugation. Compound tenses are
explained in full, as is the use of the passive. Defective verbs and 'regular'
spelling irregularities are listed and the glossary on page 9 gives
invaluable help in describing the major verb categories.

The second section – the main part of the book – shows, in alphabetical
order, each of 112 verb models, fully conjugated. Each verb model is
clearly laid out across two pages with the learning points highlighted in
colour – no more searching for where the stem ends and the ending
begins. You can see at a glance which verb ending to use for which tense
and which person. Major constructions and idiomatic phrases are given
for most verb models and similarly conjugated verbs are listed, with their
translations, for numerous verb types.

Finally, the third section of the book is an alphabetical index of over
2,000 common verbs, each one cross-referred to its basic model.

CONTENTS

THE FRENCH VERB

The majority of verbs are regular and conform to rules; the fact that irregular verbs do not follow any overall pattern means that they have to be learned individually.

The infinitive ending of regular verbs indicates to which conjugation or group they belong:
1st   conjugation: ER ending; model: DONNER (36)★
2nd conjugation: IR ending; model: FINIR (45)★
3rd conjugation: RE ending; model VENDRE (107)★
(★ = verb model number, not page number)

To conjugate a regular verb, you must add the appropriate verb ending to the appropriate tense stem. The stem for the present, imperfect, past historic and both subjunctive tenses is the infinitive minus its ER, IR or RE ending; the stem for the future and conditional tenses is the whole infinitive in the 1st and 2nd conjugations, and the infinitive minus its final E in the 3rd conjugation.

For each conjugation, the following tables show
   (1) the verb endings for each tense
   (2) how these are added to the stem.

Pr = present; I = imperfect; F = future; C = conditional; PH = past historic; PrS = present subjunctive; PS = past subjunctive

1st conjugation (1)

Tense	Endings					
Pr	e	es	e	ons	ez	ent
I	ais	ais	ait	ions	iez	aient
F	ai	as	a	ons	ez	ont
C	ais	ais	ait	ions	iez	aient
PH	ai	as	a	âmes	âtes	èrent
PrS	e	es	e	ions	iez	ent
PS	asse	asses	ât	assions	assiez	assent

(2)

	STEM	Pr	I	PH	Pr S	P S
je	donn	e	ais	ai	e	asse
tu	donn	es	ais	as	es	asses
il	donn	e	ait	a	e	ât
nous	donn	ons	ions	âmes	ions	assions
vous	donn	ez	iez	âtes	iez	assiez
ils	donn	ent	aient	èrent	ent	assent

	STEM	F	C
je	donner	ai	ais
tu	donner	as	ais
il	donner	a	ait
nous	donner	ons	ions
vous	donner	ez	iez
ils	donner	ont	aient

2nd conjugation (1)

Tense	Endings					
Pr	is	is	it	issons	issez	issent
I	issais	issais	issait	issions	issiez	issaient
F	ai	as	a	ons	ez	ont
C	ais	ais	ait	ions	iez	aient
PH	is	is	it	îmes	îtes	irent
PrS	isse	isses	isse	issions	issiez	issent
PS	isse	isses	it	issions	issiez	issent

(2)

	STEM	Pr	I	PH	Pr S	P S
je	fin	is	issais	is	isse	isse
tu	fin	is	issais	is	isses	isses
il	fin	it	issait	it	isse	ît
nous	fin	issons	issions	îmes	issions	issions
vous	fin	issez	issiez	îtes	issiez	issiez
ils	fin	issent	issaient	irent	issent	issent

	STEM	F	C
je	finir	ai	ais
tu	finir	as	ais
il	finir	a	ait
nous	finir	ons	ions
vous	finir	ez	iez
ils	finir	ont	aient

3rd conjugation (1)

Tense	Endings					
Pr	s	s	—	ons	ez	ent
I	ais	ais	ait	ions	iez	aient
F	ai	as	a	ons	ez	ont
C	ais	ais	ait	ions	iez	aient
PH	is	is	it	îmes	îtes	irent
PrS	e	es	e	ions	iez	ent
PS	isse	isses	it	issions	issiez	issent

(2)

	STEM	Pr	I	PH	Pr S	P S
je	vend	s	ais	is	e	isse
tu	vend	s	ais	is	es	isses
il	vend		ait	it	e	ît
nous	vend	ons	ions	îmes	ions	issions
vous	vend	ez	iez	îtes	iez	issiez
ils	vend	ent	aient	irent	ent	issent

	STEM	F	C
je	vendr	ai	ais
tu	vendr	as	ais
il	vendr	a	ait
nous	vendr	ons	ions
vous	vendr	ez	iez
ils	vendr	ont	aient

THE PRESENT PARTICIPLE

To form the present participle, add the following endings to the infinitive minus its ER, IR or RE ending
- 1st conjugation **ant**   (donnant)
- 2nd conjugation **issant** (finissant)
- 3rd conjugation **ant**   (vendant)

With the exception of 'en', French uses an infinitive after prepositions where English uses a present participle.
Thus: sans parler = without speaking
     après être parti = after having left
but: en faisant = while doing.

THE PAST PARTICIPLE

To form the past participle, add the following endings to the infinitive minus its ER, IR or RE ending
- 1st conjugation **é** (donné)
- 2nd conjugation **i** (fini)
- 3rd conjugation **u** (vendu)

For agreement rules in compound tenses, see p. 10.

THE IMPERATIVE

The imperative is the same as the present tense 'tu', 'nous' and 'vous' forms minus the subject pronouns: finis, allons, commencez.

Exceptions
1) ER verbs and verbs like cueillir, ouvrir etc, which keep the 's' ending of the 'tu' form only if it is immediately followed by y or en: avance, va; vas-y, cueilles-en.
2) avoir and être, whose imperative forms are the same as the present subjunctive (minus the 's' of 'tu' form for avoir).
3) vouloir: veuille, veuillons, veuillez.
4) savoir: sache, sachons, sachez.

Affirmative/negative imperative – pronoun object follows/precedes verb: prends-le/ne le prends pas; asseyez-vous/ne vous asseyez pas.

'REGULAR' SPELLING IRREGULARITIES

A number of spelling changes affect 1st conjugation verbs. Such changes and when they occur are shown below. Verb types are divided according to their infinitive ending. We suggest that you use the table in conjunction with the numbered verb models indicated. C = consonant(s).

-eler/-eter (*i: appeler 4/jeter 50; ii: acheter 1*) *either* i) l→ll/t→tt *or* ii) e→è	*before* e, es, ent; *throughout future and conditional tenses*
e + C + er (*lever 52*) e→è	*as above*
-éger (*protéger 80*) é→è; *see* **-ger**	*before* e, es, ent; *as for* **-ger**
-é + C + er (*espérer 41*) é→è	*before* e, es, ent
-oyer/-uyer (*nettoyer 63*) y→i	*before* e, es, ent; *throughout future and conditional tenses*
-ayer (*i: payer 70; ii: as for nettoyer 63*) *either* i) y retained throughout *or* ii) y→i	*as above*

-cer (*commencer 15*)
    c→ç
    (to soften c)
	when verb endings starting with a or o immediately follow c

-ger (*manger 54*)
    e retained
    (to soften g)
	when verb endings starting with a or o immediately follow g

GLOSSARY

You should familiarize yourself with the following descriptions of major verb categories.

Transitive taking a direct object
Intransitive used without a direct object
★ A verb may be transitive in English yet intransitive in French
  (and vice versa):
  he disobeyed the rules (transitive)
  il a désobéi aux règles (intransitive)
  he looked at his sister (intransitive)
  il a regardé sa sœur (transitive)

Reflexive taking a reflexive pronoun (English: myself,
               ourselves etc; French: me, nous etc) which 'reflects'
               back to the subject
★ 1) Not all verbs which are reflexive in French are reflexive in
     English
e.g. se coucher = to go to bed
  2) The reflexive pronoun is sometimes optional in English
     e.g. se laver = to wash (oneself)

Reciprocal taking a reciprocal pronoun which expresses
               mutual action or relation
               e.g. ils se regardent = they look at each other *or* one
               another
★ Since the plural forms of reciprocal and reflexive verbs are
  identical, 'ils se regardent' might mean 'they look at
  themselves'. Always gauge the correct translation from the
  context.

Auxiliary used to conjugate verbs in their compound tenses
               (see p. 10)

Impersonal used only in the 3rd person singular, to represent a
               neutral subject
               e.g. il pleut = it's raining

COMPOUND TENSES: THE USE OF AUXILIARY VERBS

In simple tenses, the verb is expressed in one word (e.g. donne, finira, vendions); in compound tenses, the past participle is added to the appropriate tense of the auxiliary verbs avoir and être (e.g. a donné, aura fini, avions vendu). Most verbs are conjugated with avoir, but the être auxiliary is used with reflexive and reciprocal verbs, and when the verb is in the passive voice. (See note on Passive: p. 12)

The following intransitive verbs are also conjugated with être:

aller	revenir	passer★
venir	retourner★	rester
entrer★	rentrer★	devenir
sortir★	monter★	naître
arriver	descendre★	mourir
partir	tomber	

(★ = conjugated with avoir when transitive)

RULES OF AGREEMENT FOR PAST PARTICIPLES

(a) The past participle of a verb conjugated with être agrees in number and gender with its subject.

Thus: elle est partie = she left

elle s'est souvenue[1] = she remembered

([1]typical of verbs which are reflexive in form but whose pronouns have no true reflexive value)

Exceptions: 1) reflexives 2) reciprocals

e.g. 1) elle s'est lavée (transitive)

elle s'est parlé (intransitive)

2) ils se sont regardés (transitive)

ils se sont parlé (intransitive)

(Exceptions explained in (b))

(b) The past participle of a verb conjugated with avoir and of a transitive reflexive or reciprocal verb agrees in number and gender with its direct object, provided the direct object precedes the verb; otherwise, the past participle remains invariable.

Thus: je les ai vendus = I sold them
      elle s'est lavée = she washed
      ils se sont regardés = they looked at each other

but: j'ai vendu les sacs = I sold the bags
      elle s'est parlé = she talked to herself
      (s' = indirect object)
      ils se sont parlé = they talked to each other
      (se = indirect object)
      (*NB*: elle s'est lavé les mains = she washed her hands – no agreement since direct object (les mains) follows the verb and s' = indirect object)

Some intransitive verbs (e.g. coûter, peser etc) may be accompanied by a complement of price, weight etc. Do not mistake this for a direct object: the past participle remains invariable – 'les 5 F que ça m'a coûté = the 5 F it cost me'; 'les 3 kilos que le colis a pesé = the 3 kilos the parcel weighed'. Also invariable are the past participles of impersonal verbs – 'les accidents qu'il y a eu = the accidents there were'.

For verbal constructions of the type 'I saw her leave', 'she heard them being scolded' (verbs of perception), or 'he took us swimming', which are translated in French by a verb plus infinitive, the rules of agreement are as follows:
1) if the preceding direct object is the subject of the infinitive, the past participle agrees in number and gender with it:
      je l'ai vue partir = I saw her leave
      il nous a emmenés nager = he took us swimming
2) if the preceding direct object is the object of the infinitive, the past participle remains invariable:
      elle les a entendu gronder
      = she heard them being scolded.

In constructions such as 'laisser faire' where laisser is used in conjunction with an infinitive, the same rules apply:
1) je les ai laissés tomber = I dropped them
2) elle s'est laissé persuader = she let herself be persuaded.

When faire is used in this way, however, it contradicts the 1st rule: the past participle remains invariable in both cases:
1) la femme qu'il a fait venir = the women he sent for
2) la montre qu'il a fait réparer = the watch he (has) had repaired.

THE PASSIVE VOICE

A transitive verb is active when its subject performs the action (she disobeyed the rules) and passive when its subject receives the action (she was punished). In French, the passive is formed by adding the past participle to the appropriate tense of être: 'elle était punie = she was punished' (note agreement with subject).

(*NB*: do not confuse a passive verb with an intransitive verb, which can only be used in the active voice –
  elle était allée = she had gone)

French does not use the passive as extensively as English, preferring
either 1) 'on': on m'a dit que ... = I was told that ...
or   2) a reflexive verb with an inanimate subject:
         ce mot ne s'emploie plus = this word is no longer used.

Note
In the tables on the following pages these abbreviations are used.

qch	quelque chose
qn	quelqu'un
sb	somebody
sth	something

DEFECTIVE VERBS

Defective verbs have missing or obsolete parts. The forms shown below are those most likely to occur. Unless otherwise stated, the auxiliary verb (where applicable) is avoir.

1 Present Participle *2* Past Participle *3* Present *4* Imperfect
5 Future *6* Conditional *7* Past Historic *8* Present Subjunctive
9 Past Subjunctive

accroire en faire accroire
apparoir *3* il appert
béer *1* béant *3* il bée *4* il béait
choir (être) *2* chu *3* chois, chois, choit, choient *5* choirai *etc*
   6 choirais *etc* *7* il chaut *9* il chût
déchoir *2* déchu *3* déchois, déchois, déchoit, déchoyons,
   déchoyez, déchoient *5* déchoirai *etc* *6* déchoirais *etc* *7* déchus
   etc *8* déchoie *etc* *9* déchusse *etc*
échoir (être) *1* échéant *2* échu *3* il échoit *5* il échoira *6* il
   échoirait *7* il échut *8* il échoie *9* il échût
faillir *1* faillant *2* failli *5* faillirai *etc* *6* faillirais *etc* *7* faillis *etc*
   NB: j'ai failli tomber = I nearly fell
gésir *1* gisant *3* gis, gis, gît, gisons, gisez *4* gisais *etc*
messeoir *1* messéant *3* il messied, ils messiéent *6* il messiérait,
   ils messiéraient
oindre *1* oignant *2* oint *3* il oint *4* il oignait
ouïr *2* ouï
paître *1* paissant *3* pais, pais, paît, paissons, paissez, paissent
   4 paissais *etc* *5* paîtrai *etc* *6* paîtrais *etc* *8* paisse *etc*
poindre *2* point *3* il point *5* il poindra
repaître *like* **paître** *but also has* *2* repu *7* repus *etc* *9* repusse *etc*
seoir (= *to become*) *1* seyant *3* il sied, ils siéent *4* il seyait, ils
   seyaient *5* il siéra, ils siéront *6* il siérait, ils siéraient *8* il siée

13

1 acheter
to buy

also **congeler**
to freeze

PRESENT PARTICIPLE
achetant

déceler
to discover

PAST PARTICIPLE
acheté

geler
to freeze

PRESENT
j'	**achète**
tu	**achètes**
il	**achète**
nous	**achetons**
vous	**achetez**
ils	**achètent**

IMPERFECT
j'	**achetais**
tu	**achetais**
il	**achetait**
nous	**achetions**
vous	**achetiez**
ils	**achetaient**

FUTURE
j'	**achèterai**
tu	**achèteras**
il	**achètera**
nous	**achèterons**
vous	**achèterez**
ils	**achèteront**

IMPERATIVE
achète
achetons
achetez

CONDITIONAL
j'	**achèterais**
tu	**achèterais**
il	**achèterait**
nous	**achèterions**
vous	**achèteriez**
ils	**achèteraient**

to buy

haleter
to paint

peler
to peel

PAST HISTORIC		PRESENT SUBJUNCTIVE	
j'	**achetai**	j'	**achète**
tu	**achetas**	tu	**achètes**
il	**acheta**	il	**achète**
nous	**achetâmes**	nous	**achetions**
vous	**achetâtes**	vous	**achetiez**
ils	**achetèrent**	ils	**achètent**

PERFECT		PAST SUBJUNCTIVE	
j'	**ai acheté**	j'	**achetasse**
tu	**as acheté**	tu	**achetasses**
il	**a acheté**	il	**achetât**
nous	**avons acheté**	nous	**achetassions**
vous	**avez acheté**	vous	**achetassiez**
ils	**ont acheté**	ils	**achetassent**

CONSTRUCTIONS
acheter qch à qn   to buy sth from sb; to buy sth for sb
je le lui ai acheté   I bought it from him; I bought it for him
je le lui ai acheté 10 F   I bought it from him for 10 F

2 acquérir
to acquire

also **conquérir**
to conquer

PRESENT PARTICIPLE
acquérant

s'enquérir
to inquire

PAST PARTICIPLE
acquis

requérir
to require

PRESENT		IMPERFECT	
j'	**acquiers**	j'	**acquérais**
tu	**acquiers**	tu	**acquérais**
il	**acquiert**	il	**acquérait**
nous	**acquérons**	nous	**acquérions**
vous	**acquérez**	vous	**acquériez**
ils	**acquièrent**	ils	**acquéraient**

FUTURE

j'	**acquerrai**
tu	**acquerras**
il	**acquerra**
nous	**acquerrons**
vous	**acquerrez**
ils	**acquerront**

IMPERATIVE	CONDITIONAL	
acquiers	j'	**acquerrais**
acquérons	tu	**acquerrais**
acquérez	il	**acquerrait**
	nous	**acquerrions**
	vous	**acquerriez**
	ils	**acquerraient**

PAST HISTORIC		PRESENT SUBJUNCTIVE	
j'	acquis	j'	acquière
tu	acquis	tu	acquières
il	acquit	il	acquière
nous	acquîmes	nous	acquérions
vous	acquîtes	vous	acquériez
ils	acquirent	ils	acquièrent
PERFECT		PAST SUBJUNCTIVE	
j'	ai acquis	j'	acquisse
tu	as acquis	tu	acquisses
il	a acquis	il	acquit
nous	avons acquis	nous	acquissions
vous	avez acquis	vous	acquissiez
ils	ont acquis	ils	acquissent

CONSTRUCTIONS

acquérir de l'expérience   to gain experience
acquérir de la valeur   to go up in value
les mauvaises habitudes s'acquièrent facilement   bad
habits are easily picked up

3 aller
to go

PRESENT PARTICIPLE
allant

PAST PARTICIPLE
allé

PRESENT		IMPERFECT	
je	**vais**	j'	**allais**
tu	**vas**	tu	**allais**
il	**va**	il	**allait**
nous	**allons**	nous	**allions**
vous	**allez**	vous	**alliez**
ils	**vont**	ils	**allaient**

		FUTURE	
		j'	**irai**
		tu	**iras**
		il	**ira**
		nous	**irons**
		vous	**irez**
		ils	**iront**

IMPERATIVE	CONDITIONAL	
va	j'	**irais**
allons	tu	**irais**
allez	il	**irait**
	nous	**irions**
	vous	**iriez**
	ils	**iraient**

aller 3

to go

PAST HISTORIC		*PRESENT SUBJUNCTIVE*	
j'	allai	j'	aille
tu	allas	tu	ailles
il	alla	il	aille
nous	allâmes	nous	allions
vous	allâtes	vous	alliez
ils	allèrent	ils	aillent
PERFECT		*PAST SUBJUNCTIVE*	
je	suis allé	j'	allasse
tu	es allé	tu	allasses
il	est allé	il	allât
nous	sommes allés	nous	allassions
vous	êtes allé(s)	vous	allassiez
ils	sont allés	ils	allassent

CONSTRUCTIONS

aller faire qch to go and do sth
aller à qn to fit sb; to suit sb
comment allez-vous? – je vais bien / mal / mieux how are
you? – I'm well / unwell / better
s'en aller to go (away); to leave
allons-y! let's go!

4 appeler
to call

also **amonceler**
to pile up

PRESENT PARTICIPLE
appelant

épeler
to spell

PAST PARTICIPLE
appelé

jumeler
to twin

PRESENT

j'	appelle
tu	appelles
il	appelle
nous	appelons
vous	appelez
ils	appellent

IMPERFECT

j'	appelais
tu	appelais
il	appelait
nous	appelions
vous	appeliez
ils	appelaient

FUTURE

j'	appellerai
tu	appelleras
il	appellera
nous	appellerons
vous	appellerez
ils	appelleront

IMPERATIVE

appelle
appelons
appelez

CONDITIONAL

j'	appellerais
tu	appellerais
il	appellerait
nous	appellerions
vous	appelleriez
ils	appelleraient

to call

rappeler
to recall

renouveler
to renew

PAST HISTORIC

j'	**appelai**
tu	**appelas**
il	**appela**
nous	**appelâmes**
vous	**appelâtes**
ils	**appelèrent**

PRESENT SUBJUNCTIVE

j'	**appelle**
tu	**appelles**
il	**appelle**
nous	**appelions**
vous	**appeliez**
ils	**appellent**

PERFECT

j'	**ai appelé**
tu	**as appelé**
il	**a appelé**
nous	**avons appelé**
vous	**avez appelé**
ils	**ont appelé**

PAST SUBJUNCTIVE

j'	**appelasse**
tu	**appelasses**
il	**appelât**
nous	**appelassions**
vous	**appelassiez**
ils	**appelassent**

CONSTRUCTIONS

comment vous appelez-vous?   what's your name?
je m'appelle Suzanne   my name is Suzanne
appeler qn à l'aide *or* **au secours**   to call to sb for help
en appeler à   to appeal to

5 apprendre
to learn

PRESENT PARTICIPLE
apprenant

PAST PARTICIPLE
appris

PRESENT
j'	**apprends**
tu	**apprends**
il	**apprend**
nous	**apprenons**
vous	**apprenez**
ils	**apprennent**

IMPERFECT
j'	**apprenais**
tu	**apprenais**
il	**apprenait**
nous	**apprenions**
vous	**appreniez**
ils	**apprenaient**

FUTURE
j'	**apprendrai**
tu	**apprendras**
il	**apprendra**
nous	**apprendrons**
vous	**apprendrez**
ils	**apprendront**

IMPERATIVE
apprends
apprenons
apprenez

CONDITIONAL
j'	**apprendrais**
tu	**apprendrais**
il	**apprendrait**
nous	**apprendrions**
vous	**apprendriez**
ils	**apprendraient**

to learn

PAST HISTORIC		PRESENT SUBJUNCTIVE	
j'	appris	j'	apprenne
tu	appris	tu	apprennes
il	apprit	il	apprenne
nous	apprîmes	nous	apprenions
vous	apprîtes	vous	appreniez
ils	apprirent	ils	apprennent

PERFECT		PAST SUBJUNCTIVE	
j'	ai appris	j'	apprisse
tu	as appris	tu	apprisses
il	a appris	il	apprît
nous	avons appris	nous	apprissions
vous	avez appris	vous	apprissiez
ils	ont appris	ils	apprissent

CONSTRUCTIONS

apprendre à faire qch   to learn (how) to do sth
apprendre qch à qn   to teach sb sth; to tell sb sth
apprendre à qn à faire qch   to teach sb (how) to do sth
l'espagnol s'apprend facilement   Spanish is easy to learn

6 arriver
to arrive

PRESENT PARTICIPLE
arrivant

PAST PARTICIPLE
arrivé

PRESENT

j'	**arrive**
tu	**arrives**
il	**arrive**
nous	**arrivons**
vous	**arrivez**
ils	**arrivent**

IMPERFECT

j'	**arrivais**
tu	**arrivais**
il	**arrivait**
nous	**arrivions**
vous	**arriviez**
ils	**arrivaient**

FUTURE

j'	**arriverai**
tu	**arriveras**
il	**arrivera**
nous	**arriverons**
vous	**arriverez**
ils	**arriveront**

IMPERATIVE

arrive
arrivons
arrivez

CONDITIONAL

j'	**arriverais**
tu	**arriverais**
il	**arriverait**
nous	**arriverions**
vous	**arriveriez**
ils	**arriveraient**

PAST HISTORIC		*PRESENT SUBJUNCTIVE*	
j'	arrivai	j'	arrive
tu	arrivas	tu	arrives
il	arriva	il	arrive
nous	arrivâmes	nous	arrivions
vous	arrivâtes	vous	arriviez
ils	arrivèrent	ils	arrivent

PERFECT		*PAST SUBJUNCTIVE*	
je	suis arrivé	j'	arrivasse
tu	es arrivé	tu	arrivasses
il	est arrivé	il	arrivât
nous	sommes arrivés	nous	arrivassions
vous	êtes arrivé(s)	vous	arrivassiez
ils	sont arrivés	ils	arrivassent

CONSTRUCTIONS

arriver à faire qch to succeed in doing sth
ça peut arriver this may happen
il lui est arrivé un accident he's had an accident
la neige lui arrivait (jusqu')aux genoux the snow came
up to his knees

7 assaillir
to attack

PRESENT PARTICIPLE
assaillant

PAST PARTICIPLE
assailli

PRESENT		*IMPERFECT*	
j'	**assaille**	j'	**assaillais**
tu	**assailles**	tu	**assaillais**
il	**assaille**	il	**assaillait**
nous	**assaillons**	nous	**assaillions**
vous	**assaillez**	vous	**assailliez**
ils	**assaillent**	ils	**assaillaient**

		FUTURE	
		j'	**assaillirai**
		tu	**assailliras**
		il	**assaillira**
		nous	**assaillirons**
		vous	**assaillirez**
		ils	**assailliront**

IMPERATIVE		*CONDITIONAL*	
	assaille	j'	**assaillirais**
	assaillons	tu	**assaillirais**
	assaillez	il	**assaillirait**
		nous	**assaillirions**
		vous	**assailliriez**
		ils	**assailliraient**

PAST HISTORIC		PRESENT SUBJUNCTIVE	
j'	assaillis	j'	assaille
tu	assaillis	tu	assailles
il	assaillit	il	assaille
nous	assaillîmes	nous	assaillions
vous	assaillîtes	vous	assailliez
ils	assaillirent	ils	assaillent

PERFECT		PAST SUBJUNCTIVE	
j'	ai assailli	j'	assaillisse
tu	as assailli	tu	assaillisses
il	a assailli	il	assaillît
nous	avons assailli	nous	assaillissions
vous	avez assailli	vous	assaillissiez
ils	ont assailli	ils	assaillissent

CONSTRUCTIONS
on l'a assailli de questions he was bombarded with questions

8 s'asseoir
to sit down

PRESENT PARTICIPLE
s'asseyant

PAST PARTICIPLE
assis

PRESENT

je	**m'assieds**
tu	**t'assieds**
il	**s'assied**
nous	**nous asseyons**
vous	**vous asseyez**
ils	**s'asseyent**

ALTERNATIVE FORM OF PRESENT

je	**m'assois**
tu	**t'assois**
il	**s'assoit**
nous	**nous assoyons**
vous	**vous assoyez**
ils	**s'assoient**

IMPERATIVE

assieds-toi
asseyons-nous
asseyez-vous

IMPERFECT

je	**m'asseyais**
tu	**t'asseyais**
il	**s'asseyait**
nous	**nous asseyions**
vous	**vous asseyiez**
ils	**s'asseyaient**

FUTURE

je	**m'assiérai**
tu	**t'assiéras**
il	**s'assiéra**
nous	**nous assiérons**
vous	**vous assiérez**
ils	**s'assiéront**

CONDITIONAL

je	**m'assiérais**
tu	**t'assiérais**
il	**s'assiérait**
nous	**nous assiérions**
vous	**vous assiériez**
ils	**s'assiéraient**

PAST HISTORIC		*PRESENT SUBJUNCTIVE*	
je	m'assis	je	m'asseye
tu	t'assis	tu	t'asseyes
il	s'assit	il	s'asseye
nous	nous assîmes	nous	nous asseyions
vous	vous assîtes	vous	vous asseyiez
ils	s'assirent	ils	s'asseyent
PERFECT		*PAST SUBJUNCTIVE*	
je	me suis assis	je	m'assisse
tu	t'es assis	tu	t'assisses
il	s'est assis	il	s'assît
nous	nous sommes assis	nous	nous assissions
vous	vous êtes assis	vous	vous assissiez
ils	se sont assis	ils	s'assissent

CONSTRUCTIONS

veuillez vous asseoir please be seated
il s'est assis sur une chaise/par terre he sat (down) on a chair/the floor
il est assis sur une chaise/par terre he is sitting on a chair/the floor

29

9 attendre
to wait

PRESENT PARTICIPLE
attendant

PAST PARTICIPLE
attendu

PRESENT		*IMPERFECT*	
j'	**attends**	j'	**attendais**
tu	**attends**	tu	**attendais**
il	**attend**	il	**attendait**
nous	**attendons**	nous	**attendions**
vous	**attendez**	vous	**attendiez**
ils	**attendent**	ils	**attendaient**

FUTURE	
j'	**attendrai**
tu	**attendras**
il	**attendra**
nous	**attendrons**
vous	**attendrez**
ils	**attendront**

IMPERATIVE	*CONDITIONAL*	
attends	j'	**attendrais**
attendons	tu	**attendrais**
attendez	il	**attendrait**
	nous	**attendrions**
	vous	**attendriez**
	ils	**attendraient**

PAST HISTORIC		*PRESENT SUBJUNCTIVE*	
j'	**attendis**	j'	**attende**
tu	**attendis**	tu	**attendes**
il	**attendit**	il	**attende**
nous	**attendîmes**	nous	**attendions**
vous	**attendîtes**	vous	**attendiez**
ils	**attendirent**	ils	**attendent**
PERFECT		*PAST SUBJUNCTIVE*	
j'	**ai attendu**	j'	**attendisse**
tu	**as attendu**	tu	**attendisses**
il	**a attendu**	il	**attendît**
nous	**avons attendu**	nous	**attendissions**
vous	**avez attendu**	vous	**attendissiez**
ils	**ont attendu**	ils	**attendissent**

CONSTRUCTIONS

nous attendons qu'il parte we're waiting for him to leave
j'ai attendu 2 heures I waited (for) 2 hours
attends d'être plus grand wait till you're older
attendre qch de qn/qch to expect sth of sb/sth
s'attendre à qch/à faire to expect sth/to do

10 avoir
to have

PRESENT PARTICIPLE
ayant

PAST PARTICIPLE
eu

PRESENT		*IMPERFECT*	
j'	**ai**	j'	**avais**
tu	**as**	tu	**avais**
il	**a**	il	**avait**
nous	**avons**	nous	**avions**
vous	**avez**	vous	**aviez**
ils	**ont**	ils	**avaient**

		FUTURE	
		j'	**aurai**
		tu	**auras**
		il	**aura**
		nous	**aurons**
		vous	**aurez**
		ils	**auront**

IMPERATIVE	*CONDITIONAL*	
aie	j'	**aurais**
ayons	tu	**aurais**
ayez	il	**aurait**
	nous	**aurions**
	vous	**auriez**
	ils	**auraient**

PAST HISTORIC		PRESENT SUBJUNCTIVE	
j'	eus	j'	aie
tu	eus	tu	aies
il	eut	il	ait
nous	eûmes	nous	ayons
vous	eûtes	vous	ayez
ils	eurent	ils	aient

PERFECT		PAST SUBJUNCTIVE	
j'	ai eu	j'	eusse
tu	as eu	tu	eusses
il	a eu	il	eût
nous	avons eu	nous	eussions
vous	avez eu	vous	eussiez
ils	ont eu	ils	eussent

CONSTRUCTIONS

j'ai des lettres à écrire   I've got letters to write

quel âge avez-vous? – j'ai 10 ans   how old are you? – I'm 10 (years old)

avoir faim/chaud/tort   to be hungry/hot/wrong

il y a   there is; there are

il y a 10 ans   10 years ago

11 battre

to beat

PRESENT PARTICIPLE
battant

PAST PARTICIPLE
battu

also **abattre**
to pull down

combattre
to fight

débattre
to discuss

PRESENT
je	bats
tu	bats
il	bat
nous	battons
vous	battez
ils	battent

IMPERFECT
je	battais
tu	battais
il	battait
nous	battions
vous	battiez
ils	battaient

FUTURE
je	battrai
tu	battras
il	battra
nous	battrons
vous	battrez
ils	battront

IMPERATIVE
bats
battons
battez

CONDITIONAL
je	battrais
tu	battrais
il	battrait
nous	battrions
vous	battriez
ils	battraient

to beat

rabattre
to pull down

PAST HISTORIC		PRESENT SUBJUNCTIVE	
je	**batt**is	je	**batt**e
tu	**batt**is	tu	**batt**es
il	**batt**it	il	**batt**e
nous	**batt**îmes	nous	**batt**ions
vous	**batt**îtes	vous	**batt**iez
ils	**batt**irent	ils	**batt**ent

PERFECT		PAST SUBJUNCTIVE	
j'	**ai batt**u	je	**batt**isse
tu	**as batt**u	tu	**batt**isses
il	**a batt**u	il	**batt**ît
nous	**avons batt**u	nous	**batt**issions
vous	**avez batt**u	vous	**batt**issiez
ils	**ont batt**u	ils	**batt**issent

CONSTRUCTIONS
battre des mains   to clap one's hands
l'oiseau battait des ailes   the bird was flapping its wings
se battre   to fight

12 boire
to drink

PRESENT PARTICIPLE
buvant

PAST PARTICIPLE
bu

PRESENT		*IMPERFECT*	
je	**bois**	je	**buvais**
tu	**bois**	tu	**buvais**
il	**boit**	il	**buvait**
nous	**buvons**	nous	**buvions**
vous	**buvez**	vous	**buviez**
ils	**boivent**	ils	**buvaient**

		FUTURE	
		je	**boirai**
		tu	**boiras**
		il	**boira**
		nous	**boirons**
		vous	**boirez**
		ils	**boiront**

IMPERATIVE		*CONDITIONAL*	
	bois	je	**boirais**
	buvons	tu	**boirais**
	buvez	il	**boirait**
		nous	**boirions**
		vous	**boiriez**
		ils	**boiraient**

to drink

PAST HISTORIC		PRESENT SUBJUNCTIVE	
je	bus	je	**boive**
tu	bus	tu	**boives**
il	but	il	**boive**
nous	bûmes	nous	**buvions**
vous	bûtes	vous	**buviez**
ils	burent	ils	**boivent**

PERFECT		PAST SUBJUNCTIVE	
j'	**ai** bu	je	busse
tu	**as** bu	tu	busses
il	**a** bu	il	bût
nous	**avons** bu	nous	bussions
vous	**avez** bu	vous	bussiez
ils	**ont** bu	ils	bussent

CONSTRUCTIONS
boire un verre to have a drink

13 bouillir
to boil

PRESENT PARTICIPLE
bouillant

PAST PARTICIPLE
bouilli

PRESENT		IMPERFECT	
je	**bous**	je	**bouill**ais
tu	**bous**	tu	**bouill**ais
il	**bout**	il	**bouill**ait
nous	**bouill**ons	nous	**bouill**ions
vous	**bouill**ez	vous	**bouill**iez
ils	**bouill**ent	ils	**bouill**aient

FUTURE

je **bouill**irai
tu **bouill**iras
il **bouill**ira
nous **bouill**irons
vous **bouill**irez
ils **bouill**iront

IMPERATIVE

bous
bouillons
bouillez

CONDITIONAL

je **bouill**irais
tu **bouill**irais
il **bouill**irait
nous **bouill**irions
vous **bouill**iriez
ils **bouill**iraient

PAST HISTORIC		PRESENT SUBJUNCTIVE	
je	**bouillis**	je	**bouille**
tu	**bouillis**	tu	**bouilles**
il	**bouillit**	il	**bouille**
nous	**bouillîmes**	nous	**bouillions**
vous	**bouillîtes**	vous	**bouilliez**
ils	**bouillirent**	ils	**bouillent**

PERFECT		PAST SUBJUNCTIVE	
j'	**ai bouilli**	je	**bouillisse**
tu	**as bouilli**	tu	**bouillisses**
il	**a bouilli**	il	**bouillît**
nous	**avons bouilli**	nous	**bouillissions**
vous	**avez bouilli**	vous	**bouillissiez**
ils	**ont bouilli**	ils	**bouillissent**

CONSTRUCTIONS

faire bouillir de l'eau/des pommes de terre   to boil
water/potatoes

bouillir de colère/d'impatience   to seethe with
anger/impatience

14 clore

to shut

PRESENT PARTICIPLE
closant

PAST PARTICIPLE
clos

PRESENT

je	**clos**
tu	**clos**
il	**clôt**
nous	**closons**
vous	**closez**
ils	**closent**

IMPERFECT

je	**closais**
tu	**closais**
il	**closait**
nous	**closions**
vous	**closiez**
ils	**closaient**

FUTURE

je	**clorai**
tu	**cloras**
il	**clora**
nous	**clorons**
vous	**clorez**
ils	**cloront**

IMPERATIVE

not used

CONDITIONAL

je	**clorais**
tu	**clorais**
il	**clorait**
nous	**clorions**
vous	**cloriez**
ils	**cloraient**

PAST HISTORIC	PRESENT SUBJUNCTIVE	
not used	je	**close**
	tu	**closes**
	il	**close**
	nous	**closions**
	vous	**closiez**
	ils	**closent**

PERFECT		PAST SUBJUNCTIVE
j'	**ai clos**	*not used*
tu	**as clos**	
il	**a clos**	
nous	**avons clos**	
vous	**avez clos**	
ils	**ont clos**	

CONSTRUCTIONS
le débat s'est clos sur cette remarque the discussion
ended with that remark
clore le bec à qn to shut sb up

15 commencer
to begin   *also* **annoncer**
to announce

PRESENT PARTICIPLE
commençant   **avancer**
to move forward

PAST PARTICIPLE
commencé   **déplacer**
to move

PRESENT		*IMPERFECT*	
je	commence	je	commençais
tu	commences	tu	commençais
il	commence	il	commençait
nous	commençons	nous	commençions
vous	commencez	vous	commenciez
ils	commencent	ils	commençaient

		FUTURE	
		je	commencerai
		tu	commenceras
		il	commencera
		nous	commencerons
		vous	commencerez
		ils	commenceront

IMPERATIVE		*CONDITIONAL*	
	commence	je	commencerais
	commençons	tu	commencerais
	commencez	il	commencerait
		nous	commencerions
		vous	commenceriez
		ils	commenceraient

to begin

effacer
to erase

lancer
to throw

PAST HISTORIC		PRESENT SUBJUNCTIVE	
je	**commençai**	je	**commence**
tu	**commenças**	tu	**commences**
il	**commença**	il	**commence**
nous	**commençâmes**	nous	**commencions**
vous	**commençâtes**	vous	**commenciez**
ils	**commencèrent**	ils	**commencent**

PERFECT		PAST SUBJUNCTIVE	
j'	**ai commencé**	je	**commençasse**
tu	**as commencé**	tu	**commençasses**
il	**a commencé**	il	**commençât**
nous	**avons commencé**	nous	**commençassions**
vous	**avez commencé**	vous	**commençassiez**
ils	**ont commencé**	ils	**commençassent**

CONSTRUCTIONS

commencer à *or* **de faire**   to begin to do
commencer par qch   to begin with sth
commencer par faire qch   to begin by doing sth
il commence à pleuvoir   it's beginning to rain

16 comprendre
to understand

PRESENT PARTICIPLE
comprenant

PAST PARTICIPLE
compris

PRESENT		*IMPERFECT*	
je	**comprends**	je	**comprenais**
tu	**comprends**	tu	**comprenais**
il	**comprend**	il	**comprenait**
nous	**comprenons**	nous	**comprenions**
vous	**comprenez**	vous	**compreniez**
ils	**comprennent**	ils	**comprenaient**

		FUTURE	
		je	**comprendrai**
		tu	**comprendras**
		il	**comprendra**
		nous	**comprendrons**
		vous	**comprendrez**
		ils	**comprendront**

IMPERATIVE	*CONDITIONAL*	
comprends	je	**comprendrais**
comprenons	tu	**comprendrais**
comprenez	il	**comprendrait**
	nous	**comprendrions**
	vous	**comprendriez**
	ils	**comprendraient**

PAST HISTORIC		PRESENT SUBJUNCTIVE	
je	compris	je	comprenne
tu	compris	tu	comprennes
il	comprit	il	comprenne
nous	comprîmes	nous	comprenions
vous	comprîtes	vous	compreniez
ils	comprirent	ils	comprennent

PERFECT		PAST SUBJUNCTIVE	
j'	ai compris	je	comprisse
tu	as compris	tu	comprisses
il	a compris	il	comprît
nous	avons compris	nous	comprissions
vous	avez compris	vous	comprissiez
ils	ont compris	ils	comprissent

CONSTRUCTIONS

la maison comprend 10 pièces   the house comprises 10 rooms
mal comprendre   to misunderstand
service compris   service charge included
100 F y compris l'électricité *or* **l'électricité y comprise**   100 F including electricity

17 conclure

to conclude   *also* **exclure**
to exclude

PRESENT PARTICIPLE
concluant

PAST PARTICIPLE
conclu

PRESENT
je	**conclus**
tu	**conclus**
il	**conclut**
nous	**concluons**
vous	**concluez**
ils	**concluent**

IMPERFECT
je	**concluais**
tu	**concluais**
il	**concluait**
nous	**concluions**
vous	**concluiez**
ils	**concluaient**

FUTURE
je	**conclurai**
tu	**concluras**
il	**conclura**
nous	**conclurons**
vous	**conclurez**
ils	**concluront**

IMPERATIVE
conclus
concluons
concluez

CONDITIONAL
je	**conclurais**
tu	**conclurais**
il	**conclurait**
nous	**conclurions**
vous	**concluriez**
ils	**concluraient**

PAST HISTORIC		PRESENT SUBJUNCTIVE	
je	**conclus**	je	**conclue**
tu	**conclus**	tu	**conclues**
il	**conclut**	il	**conclue**
nous	**conclûmes**	nous	**concluions**
vous	**conclûtes**	vous	**concluiez**
ils	**conclurent**	ils	**concluent**

PERFECT		PAST SUBJUNCTIVE	
j'	**ai conclu**	je	**conclusse**
tu	**as conclu**	tu	**conclusses**
il	**a conclu**	il	**conclût**
nous	**avons conclu**	nous	**conclussions**
vous	**avez conclu**	vous	**conclussiez**
ils	**ont conclu**	ils	**conclussent**

CONSTRUCTIONS

marché conclu!   it's a deal!
j'en ai conclu qu'il était parti   I concluded that he had gone
ils ont conclu à son innocence   they concluded that he was innocent

47

18 conduire
to lead

also **éconduire**
to dismiss

PRESENT PARTICIPLE
conduisant

PAST PARTICIPLE
conduit

PRESENT
je	**conduis**
tu	**conduis**
il	**conduit**
nous	**conduisons**
vous	**conduisez**
ils	**conduisent**

IMPERFECT
je	**conduisais**
tu	**conduisais**
il	**conduisait**
nous	**conduisions**
vous	**conduisiez**
ils	**conduisaient**

FUTURE
je	**conduirai**
tu	**conduiras**
il	**conduira**
nous	**conduirons**
vous	**conduirez**
ils	**conduiront**

IMPERATIVE
conduis
conduisons
conduisez

CONDITIONAL
je	**conduirais**
tu	**conduirais**
il	**conduirait**
nous	**conduirions**
vous	**conduiriez**
ils	**conduiraient**

to lead

PAST HISTORIC
je	**conduisis**
tu	**conduisis**
il	**conduisit**
nous	**conduisîmes**
vous	**conduisîtes**
ils	**conduisirent**

PERFECT
j'	**ai conduit**
tu	**as conduit**
il	**a conduit**
nous	**avons conduit**
vous	**avez conduit**
ils	**ont conduit**

PRESENT SUBJUNCTIVE
je	**conduise**
tu	**conduises**
il	**conduise**
nous	**conduisions**
vous	**conduisiez**
ils	**conduisent**

PAST SUBJUNCTIVE
je	**conduisisse**
tu	**conduisisses**
il	**conduisît**
nous	**conduisissions**
vous	**conduisissiez**
ils	**conduisissent**

CONSTRUCTIONS

conduire qn quelque part   to take sb somewhere; to drive sb somewhere

conduire qn à faire qch   to lead sb to do sth

cet escalier conduit au toit   these stairs lead (up) to the roof

se conduire   to behave (oneself)

19 connaître

to know

PRESENT PARTICIPLE
connaissant

PAST PARTICIPLE
connu

also **méconnaître**
to be unaware of

reconnaître
to recognize

PRESENT
je	**connais**
tu	**connais**
il	**connaît**
nous	**connaissons**
vous	**connaissez**
ils	**connaissent**

IMPERFECT
je	**connaissais**
tu	**connaissais**
il	**connaissait**
nous	**connaissions**
vous	**connaissiez**
ils	**connaissaient**

FUTURE
je	**connaîtrai**
tu	**connaîtras**
il	**connaîtra**
nous	**connaîtrons**
vous	**connaîtrez**
ils	**connaîtront**

IMPERATIVE

connais
connaissons
connaissez

CONDITIONAL
je	**connaîtrais**
tu	**connaîtrais**
il	**connaîtrait**
nous	**connaîtrions**
vous	**connaîtriez**
ils	**connaîtraient**

to know

PAST HISTORIC		PRESENT SUBJUNCTIVE	
je	connus	je	connaisse
tu	connus	tu	connaisses
il	connut	il	connaisse
nous	connûmes	nous	connaissions
vous	connûtes	vous	connaissiez
ils	connurent	ils	connaissent

PERFECT		PAST SUBJUNCTIVE	
j'	ai connu	je	connusse
tu	as connu	tu	connusses
il	a connu	il	connût
nous	avons connu	nous	connussions
vous	avez connu	vous	connussiez
ils	ont connu	ils	connussent

CONSTRUCTIONS

connaître qn de vue/nom   to know sb by sight/name
il connaît bien la littérature anglaise   he's very familiar
with English literature
faire connaître qn à qn   to introduce sb to sb
se faire connaître   to make a name for oneself; to
introduce oneself

20 coudre
to sew

PRESENT PARTICIPLE
cousant

PAST PARTICIPLE
cousu

PRESENT		IMPERFECT	
je	**couds**	je	**cousais**
tu	**couds**	tu	**cousais**
il	**coud**	il	**cousait**
nous	**cousons**	nous	**cousions**
vous	**cousez**	vous	**cousiez**
ils	**cousent**	ils	**cousaient**

		FUTURE	
		je	**coudrai**
		tu	**coudras**
		il	**coudra**
		nous	**coudrons**
		vous	**coudrez**
		ils	**coudront**

IMPERATIVE		CONDITIONAL	
	couds	je	**coudrais**
	cousons	tu	**coudrais**
	cousez	il	**coudrait**
		nous	**coudrions**
		vous	**coudriez**
		ils	**coudraient**

PAST HISTORIC		*PRESENT SUBJUNCTIVE*	
je	cousis	je	couse
tu	cousis	tu	couses
il	cousit	il	couse
nous	cousîmes	nous	cousions
vous	cousîtes	vous	cousiez
ils	cousirent	ils	cousent

PERFECT		*PAST SUBJUNCTIVE*	
j'	ai cousu	je	cousisse
tu	as cousu	tu	cousisses
il	a cousu	il	cousît
nous	avons cousu	nous	cousissions
vous	avez cousu	vous	cousissiez
ils	ont cousu	ils	cousissent

CONSTRUCTIONS

coudre un bouton à une veste   to sew a button on a jacket

21 courir
to run

also **accourir**
to rush

PRESENT PARTICIPLE
courant

concourir
to compete

PAST PARTICIPLE
couru

parcourir
to go through

PRESENT	
je	**cours**
tu	**cours**
il	**court**
nous	**courons**
vous	**courez**
ils	**courent**

IMPERFECT	
je	**courais**
tu	**courais**
il	**courait**
nous	**courions**
vous	**couriez**
ils	**couraient**

FUTURE	
je	**courrai**
tu	**courras**
il	**courra**
nous	**courrons**
vous	**courrez**
ils	**courront**

IMPERATIVE
cours
courons
courez

CONDITIONAL	
je	**courrais**
tu	**courrais**
il	**courrait**
nous	**courrions**
vous	**courriez**
ils	**courraient**

courir 21
to run

secourir
to rescue

PAST HISTORIC
je	**courus**
tu	**courus**
il	**courut**
nous	**courûmes**
vous	**courûtes**
ils	**coururent**

PRESENT SUBJUNCTIVE
je	**coure**
tu	**coures**
il	**coure**
nous	**courions**
vous	**couriez**
ils	**courent**

PERFECT
j'	**ai couru**
tu	**as couru**
il	**a couru**
nous	**avons couru**
vous	**avez couru**
ils	**ont couru**

PAST SUBJUNCTIVE
je	**courusse**
tu	**courusses**
il	**courût**
nous	**courussions**
vous	**courussiez**
ils	**courussent**

CONSTRUCTIONS

courir faire qch to rush and do sth
courir à toutes jambes to run as fast as one's legs can carry one
le bruit court que ... the rumour is going round that ...
courir le risque de to run the risk of

22 couvrir

to cover · *also* **recouvrir**
to re-cover

PRESENT PARTICIPLE
couvrant

PAST PARTICIPLE
couvert

PRESENT
je	couvre
tu	couvres
il	couvre
nous	couvrons
vous	couvrez
ils	couvrent

IMPERFECT
je	couvrais
tu	couvrais
il	couvrait
nous	couvrions
vous	couvriez
ils	couvraient

FUTURE
je	couvrirai
tu	couvriras
il	couvrira
nous	couvrirons
vous	couvrirez
ils	couvriront

IMPERATIVE
couvre
couvrons
couvrez

CONDITIONAL
je	couvrirais
tu	couvrirais
il	couvrirait
nous	couvririons
vous	couvririez
ils	couvriraient

to cover

PAST HISTORIC		*PRESENT SUBJUNCTIVE*	
je	**couvris**	je	**couvre**
tu	**couvris**	tu	**couvres**
il	**couvrit**	il	**couvre**
nous	**couvrîmes**	nous	**couvrions**
vous	**couvrîtes**	vous	**couvriez**
ils	**couvrirent**	ils	**couvrent**

PERFECT		*PAST SUBJUNCTIVE*	
j'	**ai** couvert	je	**couvrisse**
tu	**as** couvert	tu	**couvrisses**
il	**a** couvert	il	**couvrît**
nous	**avons** couvert	nous	**couvrissions**
vous	**avez** couvert	vous	**couvrissiez**
ils	**ont** couvert	ils	**couvrissent**

CONSTRUCTIONS

la voiture nous a couverts de boue   the car covered us in mud

couvrir qn de cadeaux   to shower sb with gifts

elle s'est couvert le visage des mains   she covered her face with her hands

couvrez-vous bien!   wrap up well!

23 craindre
to fear

also **contraindre**
to compel

PRESENT PARTICIPLE
craignant

plaindre
to pity

PAST PARTICIPLE
craint

PRESENT		*IMPERFECT*	
je	crains	je	craignais
tu	crains	tu	craignais
il	craint	il	craignait
nous	craignons	nous	craignions
vous	craignez	vous	craigniez
ils	craignent	ils	craignaient

		FUTURE	
		je	craindrai
		tu	craindras
		il	craindra
		nous	craindrons
		vous	craindrez
		ils	craindront

IMPERATIVE		*CONDITIONAL*	
	crains	je	craindrais
	craignons	tu	craindrais
	craignez	il	craindrait
		nous	craindrions
		vous	craindriez
		ils	craindraient

PAST HISTORIC		*PRESENT SUBJUNCTIVE*	
je	**craignis**	je	**craigne**
tu	**craignis**	tu	**craignes**
il	**craignit**	il	**craigne**
nous	**craignîmes**	nous	**craignions**
vous	**craignîtes**	vous	**craigniez**
ils	**craignirent**	ils	**craignent**

PERFECT		*PAST SUBJUNCTIVE*	
j'	**ai** craint	je	**craignisse**
tu	**as** craint	tu	**craignisses**
il	**a** craint	il	**craignît**
nous	**avons** craint	nous	**craignissions**
vous	**avez** craint	vous	**craignissiez**
ils	**ont** craint	ils	**craignissent**

CONSTRUCTIONS
ne craignez rien   don't be afraid
craindre de faire qch   to be afraid of doing sth
ces plantes craignent la chaleur   these plants dislike heat

24 créer

to create

also **agréer**
   to accept

PRESENT PARTICIPLE
créant

maugréer
   to grumble

PAST PARTICIPLE
créé

procréer
   to procreate

PRESENT		*IMPERFECT*	
je	**crée**	je	**créais**
tu	**crées**	tu	**créais**
il	**crée**	il	**créait**
nous	**créons**	nous	**créions**
vous	**créez**	vous	**créiez**
ils	**créent**	ils	**créaient**

		FUTURE	
		je	**créerai**
		tu	**créeras**
		il	**créera**
		nous	**créerons**
		vous	**créerez**
		ils	**créeront**

IMPERATIVE		*CONDITIONAL*	
	crée	je	**créerais**
	créons	tu	**créerais**
	créez	il	**créerait**
		nous	**créerions**
		vous	**créeriez**
		ils	**créeraient**

récréer
to recreate

PAST HISTORIC		PRESENT SUBJUNCTIVE	
je	créai	je	crée
tu	créas	tu	crées
il	créa	il	crée
nous	créâmes	nous	créions
vous	créâtes	vous	créiez
ils	créèrent	ils	créent

PERFECT		PAST SUBJUNCTIVE	
j'	ai créé	je	créasse
tu	as créé	tu	créasses
il	a créé	il	créât
nous	avons créé	nous	créassions
vous	avez créé	vous	créassiez
ils	ont créé	ils	créassent

CONSTRUCTIONS
il nous a créé des ennuis   he's caused us problems
il s'est créé une clientèle   he has built up custom

25 crier

to shout

PRESENT PARTICIPLE
criant

PAST PARTICIPLE
crié

also **amplifier**
to amplify

associer
to associate

copier
to copy

PRESENT
je	**crie**
tu	**cries**
il	**crie**
nous	**crions**
vous	**criez**
ils	**crient**

IMPERFECT
je	**criais**
tu	**criais**
il	**criait**
nous	**criions**
vous	**criiez**
ils	**criaient**

FUTURE
je	**crierai**
tu	**crieras**
il	**criera**
nous	**crierons**
vous	**crierez**
ils	**crieront**

IMPERATIVE
crie
crions
criez

CONDITIONAL
je	**crierais**
tu	**crierais**
il	**crierait**
nous	**crierions**
vous	**crieriez**
ils	**crieraient**

étudier
to study

to shout

marier
to marry

PAST HISTORIC		PRESENT SUBJUNCTIVE	
je	criai	je	crie
tu	crias	tu	cries
il	cria	il	crie
nous	criâmes	nous	criions
vous	criâtes	vous	criiez
ils	crièrent	ils	crient

PERFECT		PAST SUBJUNCTIVE	
j'	ai crié	je	criasse
tu	as crié	tu	criasses
il	a crié	il	criât
nous	avons crié	nous	criassions
vous	avez crié	vous	criassiez
ils	ont crié	ils	criassent

CONSTRUCTIONS

crier à tue-tête   to shout one's head off
crier contre *or* **après qn**   to nag (at) sb
crier à qn de faire qch   to shout at sb to do sth
crier qch sur les toits   to proclaim sth from the rooftops
crier au secours   to shout for help

26 croire
to believe

PRESENT PARTICIPLE
croyant

PAST PARTICIPLE
cru

PRESENT
je	**crois**
tu	**crois**
il	**croit**
nous	**croyons**
vous	**croyez**
ils	**croient**

IMPERFECT
je	croyais
tu	croyais
il	croyait
nous	croyions
vous	croyiez
ils	croyaient

FUTURE
je	**croirai**
tu	**croiras**
il	**croira**
nous	**croirons**
vous	**croirez**
ils	**croiront**

IMPERATIVE
crois
croyons
croyez

CONDITIONAL
je	**croirais**
tu	**croirais**
il	**croirait**
nous	**croirions**
vous	**croiriez**
ils	**croiraient**

PAST HISTORIC		PRESENT SUBJUNCTIVE	
je	crus	je	croie
tu	crus	tu	croies
il	crut	il	croie
nous	crûmes	nous	croyions
vous	crûtes	vous	croyiez
ils	crurent	ils	croient

PERFECT		PAST SUBJUNCTIVE	
j'	ai cru	je	crusse
tu	as cru	tu	crusses
il	a cru	il	crût
nous	avons cru	nous	crussions
vous	avez cru	vous	crussiez
ils	ont cru	ils	crussent

CONSTRUCTIONS

croire aux fantômes/en Dieu   to believe in ghosts/God
on l'a cru mort   he was presumed (to be) dead
elle croyait avoir perdu son sac   she thought she had lost her bag
je crois que oui   I think so, I think we will *etc*

27 croître

to grow

PRESENT PARTICIPLE
croissant

PAST PARTICIPLE
crû (*NB*: crue, crus, crues)

PRESENT

je	**croîs**
tu	**croîs**
il	**croît**
nous	**croissons**
vous	**croissez**
ils	**croissent**

IMPERFECT

je	**croissais**
tu	**croissais**
il	**croissait**
nous	**croissions**
vous	**croissiez**
ils	**croissaient**

FUTURE

je	**croîtrai**
tu	**croîtras**
il	**croîtra**
nous	**croîtrons**
vous	**croîtrez**
ils	**croîtront**

IMPERATIVE

croîs
croissons
croissez

CONDITIONAL

je	**croîtrais**
tu	**croîtrais**
il	**croîtrait**
nous	**croîtrions**
vous	**croîtriez**
ils	**croîtraient**

to grow

PAST HISTORIC		PRESENT SUBJUNCTIVE	
je	crûs	je	croisse
tu	crûs	tu	croisses
il	crût	il	croisse
nous	crûmes	nous	croissions
vous	crûtes	vous	croissiez
ils	crûrent	ils	croissent

PERFECT		PAST SUBJUNCTIVE	
j'	ai crû	je	crûsse
tu	as crû	tu	crûsses
il	a crû	il	crût
nous	avons crû	nous	crûssions
vous	avez crû	vous	crûssiez
ils	ont crû	ils	crûssent

CONSTRUCTIONS

croître en beauté/nombre   to grow in beauty/number
les jours croissent   the days are getting longer

28 cueillir
to pick

also **accueillir**
to welcome

PRESENT PARTICIPLE
cueillant

recueillir
to collect

PAST PARTICIPLE
cueilli

PRESENT
je	**cueill**e
tu	**cueill**es
il	**cueill**e
nous	**cueill**ons
vous	**cueill**ez
ils	**cueill**ent

IMPERATIVE

cueille
cueillons
cueillez

IMPERFECT
je	**cueill**ais
tu	**cueill**ais
il	**cueill**ait
nous	**cueill**ions
vous	**cueill**iez
ils	**cueill**aient

FUTURE
je	**cueill**erai
tu	**cueill**eras
il	**cueill**era
nous	**cueill**erons
vous	**cueill**erez
ils	**cueill**eront

CONDITIONAL
je	**cueill**erais
tu	**cueill**erais
il	**cueill**erait
nous	**cueill**erions
vous	**cueill**eriez
ils	**cueill**eraient

PAST HISTORIC		*PRESENT SUBJUNCTIVE*	
je	**cueillis**	je	**cueille**
tu	**cueillis**	tu	**cueilles**
il	**cueillit**	il	**cueille**
nous	**cueillîmes**	nous	**cueillions**
vous	**cueillîtes**	vous	**cueilliez**
ils	**cueillirent**	ils	**cueillent**

PERFECT		*PAST SUBJUNCTIVE*	
j'	**ai cueilli**	je	**cueillisse**
tu	**as cueilli**	tu	**cueillisses**
il	**a cueilli**	il	**cueillît**
nous	**avons cueilli**	nous	**cueillissions**
vous	**avez cueilli**	vous	**cueillissiez**
ils	**ont cueilli**	ils	**cueillissent**

CONSTRUCTIONS
cueillir qn à froid   to catch sb off guard

29 cuire

to cook

also **construire**
to build

PRESENT PARTICIPLE
cuisant

instruire
to teach

PAST PARTICIPLE
cuit

produire
to produce

PRESENT

je	**cuis**
tu	**cuis**
il	**cuit**
nous	**cuisons**
vous	**cuisez**
ils	**cuisent**

IMPERFECT

je	**cuisais**
tu	**cuisais**
il	**cuisait**
nous	**cuisions**
vous	**cuisiez**
ils	**cuisaient**

FUTURE

je	**cuirai**
tu	**cuiras**
il	**cuira**
nous	**cuirons**
vous	**cuirez**
ils	**cuiront**

IMPERATIVE

cuis
cuisons
cuisez

CONDITIONAL

je	**cuirais**
tu	**cuirais**
il	**cuirait**
nous	**cuirions**
vous	**cuiriez**
ils	**cuiraient**

réduire
to reduce

séduire
to charm

PAST HISTORIC		PRESENT SUBJUNCTIVE	
je	cuisis	je	cuise
tu	cuisis	tu	cuises
il	cuisit	il	cuise
nous	cuisîmes	nous	cuisions
vous	cuisîtes	vous	cuisiez
ils	cuisirent	ils	cuisent

PERFECT		PAST SUBJUNCTIVE	
j'	ai cuit	je	cuisisse
tu	as cuit	tu	cuisisses
il	a cuit	il	cuisît
nous	avons cuit	nous	cuisissions
vous	avez cuit	vous	cuisissiez
ils	ont cuit	ils	cuisissent

CONSTRUCTIONS
cuire au gaz/à l'électricité to cook with gas/by electricity
cuire au four to bake; to roast
cuire à la vapeur to steam
cuire à feu doux to cook gently
bien cuit well done

30 découvrir
to discover

PRESENT PARTICIPLE
découvrant

PAST PARTICIPLE
découvert

PRESENT		*IMPERFECT*	
je	**découvre**	je	**découvr**ais
tu	**découvres**	tu	**découvr**ais
il	**découvre**	il	**découvr**ait
nous	**découvr**ons	nous	**découvr**ions
vous	**découvr**ez	vous	**découvr**iez
ils	**découvr**ent	ils	**découvr**aient

		FUTURE	
		je	**découvrir**ai
		tu	**découvrir**as
		il	**découvrir**a
		nous	**découvrir**ons
		vous	**découvrir**ez
		ils	**découvrir**ont

IMPERATIVE		*CONDITIONAL*	
découvre		je	**découvrir**ais
découvrons		tu	**découvrir**ais
découvrez		il	**découvrir**ait
		nous	**découvrir**ions
		vous	**découvrir**iez
		ils	**découvrir**aient

PAST HISTORIC		PRESENT SUBJUNCTIVE	
je	**découvris**	je	**découvre**
tu	**découvris**	tu	**découvres**
il	**découvrit**	il	**découvre**
nous	**découvrîmes**	nous	**découvrions**
vous	**découvrîtes**	vous	**découvriez**
ils	**découvrirent**	ils	**découvrent**

PERFECT		PAST SUBJUNCTIVE	
j'	**ai** découvert	je	**découvrisse**
tu	**as** découvert	tu	**découvrisses**
il	**a** découvert	il	**découvrît**
nous	**avons** découvert	nous	**découvrissions**
vous	**avez** découvert	vous	**découvrissiez**
ils	**ont** découvert	ils	**découvrissent**

CONSTRUCTIONS

il craint d'être découvert   he's afraid of being found out
une robe qui découvre les épaules   a dress which reveals the shoulders
se découvrir   to take off one's hat; to undress

31 descendre
to go down

PRESENT PARTICIPLE
descendant

PAST PARTICIPLE
descendu

PRESENT		*IMPERFECT*	
je	**descends**	je	**descendais**
tu	**descends**	tu	**descendais**
il	**descend**	il	**descendait**
nous	**descendons**	nous	**descendions**
vous	**descendez**	vous	**descendiez**
ils	**descendent**	ils	**descendaient**

		FUTURE	
		je	**descendrai**
		tu	**descendras**
		il	**descendra**
		nous	**descendrons**
		vous	**descendrez**
		ils	**descendront**

IMPERATIVE	*CONDITIONAL*	
descends	je	**descendrais**
descendons	tu	**descendrais**
descendez	il	**descendrait**
	nous	**descendrions**
	vous	**descendriez**
	ils	**descendraient**

to go down

PAST HISTORIC		PRESENT SUBJUNCTIVE	
je	**descendis**	je	**descende**
tu	**descendis**	tu	**descendes**
il	**descendit**	il	**descende**
nous	**descendîmes**	nous	**descendions**
vous	**descendîtes**	vous	**descendiez**
ils	**descendirent**	ils	**descendent**

PERFECT		PAST SUBJUNCTIVE	
je	suis **descendu**	je	**descendisse**
tu	es **descendu**	tu	**descendisses**
il	est **descendu**	il	**descendît**
nous	sommes	nous	**descendissions**
	descendus	vous	**descendissiez**
vous	êtes **descendu(s)**	ils	**descendissent**
ils	sont **descendus**		

CONSTRUCTIONS

descendre de voiture/du train/de bicyclette to get out of the car/off the train/off one's bicycle
sa jupe lui descend jusqu'aux chevilles her skirt comes down to her ankles
il a descendu la valise he took the case down

32 détruire
to destroy

PRESENT PARTICIPLE
détruisant

PAST PARTICIPLE
détruit

PRESENT
je	**détruis**
tu	**détruis**
il	**détruit**
nous	**détruisons**
vous	**détruisez**
ils	**détruisent**

IMPERFECT
je	**détruisais**
tu	**détruisais**
il	**détruisait**
nous	**détruisions**
vous	**détruisiez**
ils	**détruisaient**

FUTURE
je	**détruirai**
tu	**détruiras**
il	**détruira**
nous	**détruirons**
vous	**détruirez**
ils	**détruiront**

IMPERATIVE
détruis
détruisons
détruisez

CONDITIONAL
je	**détruirais**
tu	**détruirais**
il	**détruirait**
nous	**détruirions**
vous	**détruiriez**
ils	**détruiraient**

PAST HISTORIC		PRESENT SUBJUNCTIVE	
je	**détrui**sis	je	**détrui**se
tu	**détrui**sis	tu	**détrui**ses
il	**détrui**sit	il	**détrui**se
nous	**détrui**sîmes	nous	**détrui**sions
vous	**détrui**sîtes	vous	**détrui**siez
ils	**détrui**sirent	ils	**détrui**sent

PERFECT		PAST SUBJUNCTIVE	
j'	**ai détrui**t	je	**détrui**sisse
tu	**as détrui**t	tu	**détrui**sisses
il	**a détrui**t	il	**détrui**sît
nous	**avons détrui**t	nous	**détrui**sissions
vous	**avez détrui**t	vous	**détrui**sissiez
ils	**ont détrui**t	ils	**détrui**sissent

CONSTRUCTIONS
détruire par le feu   to destroy by fire

33 devenir
to become

PRESENT PARTICIPLE
devenant

PAST PARTICIPLE
devenu

PRESENT

je	deviens
tu	deviens
il	devient
nous	**deven**ons
vous	**deven**ez
ils	deviennent

IMPERFECT

je	**deven**ais
tu	**deven**ais
il	**deven**ait
nous	**deven**ions
vous	**deven**iez
ils	**deven**aient

FUTURE

je	**deviendr**ai
tu	**deviendr**as
il	**deviendr**a
nous	**deviendr**ons
vous	**deviendr**ez
ils	**deviendr**ont

IMPERATIVE

deviens
devenons
devenez

CONDITIONAL

je	**deviendr**ais
tu	**deviendr**ais
il	**deviendr**ait
nous	**deviendr**ions
vous	**deviendr**iez
ils	**deviendr**aient

PAST HISTORIC		*PRESENT SUBJUNCTIVE*	
je	devins	je	devienne
tu	devins	tu	deviennes
il	devint	il	devienne
nous	devînmes	nous	**deven**ions
vous	devîntes	vous	**deven**iez
ils	devinrent	ils	deviennent

PERFECT		*PAST SUBJUNCTIVE*	
je	suis **deven**u	je	devinsse
tu	es **deven**u	tu	devinsses
il	est **deven**u	il	devînt
nous	sommes **deven**us	nous	devinssions
vous	êtes **deven**u(s)	vous	devinssiez
ils	sont **deven**us	ils	devinssent

CONSTRUCTIONS

devenir médecin/professeur   to become a doctor/a teacher

devenir vieux/grand   to get old/tall

qu'est-il devenu?   what has become of him?

il devient de plus en plus agressif   he's growing increasingly aggressive

34 devoir

to have to; to owe

PRESENT PARTICIPLE
devant

PAST PARTICIPLE
dû (*NB*: **due, dus, dues**)

PRESENT
je	**dois**
tu	**dois**
il	**doit**
nous	**dev**ons
vous	**dev**ez
ils	**doivent**

IMPERFECT
je	**dev**ais
tu	**dev**ais
il	**dev**ait
nous	**dev**ions
vous	**dev**iez
ils	**dev**aient

FUTURE
je	**dev**rai
tu	**dev**ras
il	**dev**ra
nous	**dev**rons
vous	**dev**rez
ils	**dev**ront

IMPERATIVE
dois
devons
devez

CONDITIONAL
je	**dev**rais
tu	**dev**rais
il	**dev**rait
nous	**dev**rions
vous	**dev**riez
ils	**dev**raient

PAST HISTORIC		PRESENT SUBJUNCTIVE	
je	dus	je	doive
tu	dus	tu	doives
il	dut	il	doive
nous	dûmes	nous	**dev**ions
vous	dûtes	vous	**dev**iez
ils	dûrent	ils	doivent

PERFECT		PAST SUBJUNCTIVE	
j'	**ai** dû	je	dusse
tu	**as** dû	tu	dusses
il	**a** dû	il	dût
nous	**avons** dû	nous	dussions
vous	**avez** dû	vous	dussiez
ils	**ont** dû	ils	dussent

CONSTRUCTIONS

devoir qch à qn   to owe sb sth
devoir faire qch   to have to do sth
il doit arriver ce soir   he is due (to arrive) tonight
il a dû s'égarer   he must have got lost
ceci est dû à ...   this is due to ...

35 dire
to say

PRESENT PARTICIPLE
disant

PAST PARTICIPLE
dit

PRESENT		*IMPERFECT*	
je	**dis**	je	**disais**
tu	**dis**	tu	**disais**
il	**dit**	il	**disait**
nous	**disons**	nous	**disions**
vous	**dites**	vous	**disiez**
ils	**disent**	ils	**disaient**

FUTURE

je	**dirai**
tu	**diras**
il	**dira**
nous	**dirons**
vous	**direz**
ils	**diront**

IMPERATIVE

dis
disons
dites

CONDITIONAL

je	**dirais**
tu	**dirais**
il	**dirait**
nous	**dirions**
vous	**diriez**
ils	**diraient**

to say

PAST HISTORIC

je	dis
tu	dis
il	dit
nous	dîmes
vous	dîtes
ils	dirent

PRESENT SUBJUNCTIVE

je	dise
tu	dises
il	dise
nous	disions
vous	disiez
ils	disent

PERFECT

j'	**ai** dit
tu	**as** dit
il	**a** dit
nous	**avons** dit
vous	**avez** dit
ils	**ont** dit

PAST SUBJUNCTIVE

je	disse
tu	disses
il	dît
nous	dissions
vous	dissiez
ils	dissent

CONSTRUCTIONS
dire qch à qn to tell sb sth
dire à qn de faire qch to tell sb to do sth
cela ne me dit rien I don't fancy it
on dirait du poulet it tastes like chicken
on dirait Jean it looks like John

36 donner

to give · *also* **accepter**
to accept

PRESENT PARTICIPLE
donnant

causer
to cause

PAST PARTICIPLE
donné

laver
to wash

PRESENT
je	**donne**
tu	**donnes**
il	**donne**
nous	**donnons**
vous	**donnez**
ils	**donnent**

IMPERFECT
je	**donnais**
tu	**donnais**
il	**donnait**
nous	**donnions**
vous	**donniez**
ils	**donnaient**

FUTURE
je	**donnerai**
tu	**donneras**
il	**donnera**
nous	**donnerons**
vous	**donnerez**
ils	**donneront**

IMPERATIVE
donne
donnons
donnez

CONDITIONAL
je	**donnerais**
tu	**donnerais**
il	**donnerait**
nous	**donnerions**
vous	**donneriez**
ils	**donneraient**

to give

poser
to put

rêver
to dream

PAST HISTORIC		PRESENT SUBJUNCTIVE	
je	**donn**ai	je	**donne**
tu	**donn**as	tu	**donnes**
il	**donn**a	il	**donne**
nous	**donn**âmes	nous	**donnions**
vous	**donn**âtes	vous	**donniez**
ils	**donn**èrent	ils	**donnent**

PERFECT		PAST SUBJUNCTIVE	
j'	**ai donné**	je	**donnasse**
tu	**as donné**	tu	**donnasses**
il	**a donné**	il	**donnât**
nous	**avons donné**	nous	**donnassions**
vous	**avez donné**	vous	**donnassiez**
ils	**ont donné**	ils	**donnassent**

CONSTRUCTIONS

donner qch à qn   to give sb sth
donner quelque chose à faire à qn   to give sb something to do
donner à boire à qn   to give sb something to drink
cela me donne soif   this makes me (feel) thirsty
donner sur   to open onto; to overlook

37 dormir
to sleep

also s'endormir
to fall asleep

PRESENT PARTICIPLE
dormant

PAST PARTICIPLE
dormi

PRESENT		*IMPERFECT*	
je	**dors**	je	**dormais**
tu	**dors**	tu	**dormais**
il	**dort**	il	**dormait**
nous	**dormons**	nous	**dormions**
vous	**dormez**	vous	**dormiez**
ils	**dorment**	ils	**dormaient**

		FUTURE	
		je	**dormirai**
		tu	**dormiras**
		il	**dormira**
		nous	**dormirons**
		vous	**dormirez**
		ils	**dormiront**

IMPERATIVE		*CONDITIONAL*	
	dors	je	**dormirais**
	dormons	tu	**dormirais**
	dormez	il	**dormirait**
		nous	**dormirions**
		vous	**dormiriez**
		ils	**dormiraient**

dormir 37
to sleep

PAST HISTORIC		PRESENT SUBJUNCTIVE	
je	**dormis**	je	**dorme**
tu	**dormis**	tu	**dormes**
il	**dormit**	il	**dorme**
nous	**dormîmes**	nous	**dormions**
vous	**dormîtes**	vous	**dormiez**
ils	**dormirent**	ils	**dorment**

PERFECT		PAST SUBJUNCTIVE	
j'	**ai dormi**	je	**dormisse**
tu	**as dormi**	tu	**dormisses**
il	**a dormi**	il	**dormît**
nous	**avons dormi**	nous	**dormissions**
vous	**avez dormi**	vous	**dormissiez**
ils	**ont dormi**	ils	**dormissent**

CONSTRUCTIONS
il dort he's asleep
j'ai mal dormi I didn't sleep well
il dort d'un sommeil léger he's a light sleeper
je n'ai pas dormi de la nuit I didn't sleep a wink (all night)

38 écrire
to write

also décrire
to describe

PRESENT PARTICIPLE
écrivant

inscrire
to write

PAST PARTICIPLE
écrit

souscrire
to subscribe

PRESENT

j'	écris
tu	écris
il	écrit
nous	écrivons
vous	écrivez
ils	écrivent

IMPERFECT

j'	écrivais
tu	écrivais
il	écrivait
nous	écrivions
vous	écriviez
ils	écrivaient

FUTURE

j'	écrirai
tu	écriras
il	écrira
nous	écrirons
vous	écrirez
ils	écriront

IMPERATIVE

écris
écrivons
écrivez

CONDITIONAL

j'	écrirais
tu	écrirais
il	écrirait
nous	écririons
vous	écririez
ils	écriraient

transcrire
to transcribe

PAST HISTORIC		PRESENT SUBJUNCTIVE	
j'	**écrivis**	j'	**écrive**
tu	**écrivis**	tu	**écrives**
il	**écrivit**	il	**écrive**
nous	**écrivîmes**	nous	**écrivions**
vous	**écrivîtes**	vous	**écriviez**
ils	**écrivirent**	ils	**écrivent**

PERFECT		PAST SUBJUNCTIVE	
j'	**ai écrit**	j'	**écrivisse**
tu	**as écrit**	tu	**écrivisses**
il	**a écrit**	il	**écrivît**
nous	**avons écrit**	nous	**écrivissions**
vous	**avez écrit**	vous	**écrivissiez**
ils	**ont écrit**	ils	**écrivissent**

CONSTRUCTIONS

écrit à la main/à la machine handwritten/typed
appeler s'écrit avec deux p appeler is spelt with two ps

39 entrer

to enter

PRESENT PARTICIPLE
entrant

PAST PARTICIPLE
entré

PRESENT

j'	**entre**
tu	**entres**
il	**entre**
nous	**entrons**
vous	**entrez**
ils	**entrent**

IMPERFECT

j'	**entrais**
tu	**entrais**
il	**entrait**
nous	**entrions**
vous	**entriez**
ils	**entraient**

FUTURE

j'	**entrerai**
tu	**entreras**
il	**entrera**
nous	**entrerons**
vous	**entrerez**
ils	**entreront**

IMPERATIVE

entre
entrons
entrez

CONDITIONAL

j'	**entrerais**
tu	**entrerais**
il	**entrerait**
nous	**entrerions**
vous	**entreriez**
ils	**entreraient**

PAST HISTORIC		*PRESENT SUBJUNCTIVE*	
j'	**entrai**	j'	**entre**
tu	**entras**	tu	**entres**
il	**entra**	il	**entre**
nous	**entrâmes**	nous	**entrions**
vous	**entrâtes**	vous	**entriez**
ils	**entrèrent**	ils	**entrent**

PERFECT		*PAST SUBJUNCTIVE*	
je	suis **entré**	j'	**entrasse**
tu	es **entré**	tu	**entrasses**
il	est **entré**	il	**entrât**
nous	sommes **entrés**	nous	**entrassions**
vous	êtes **entré(s)**	vous	**entrassiez**
ils	sont **entrés**	ils	**entrassent**

CONSTRUCTIONS

entrer dans une pièce/une voiture   to go (*or* come) into a room/get into a car

faire entrer qn   to show *or* ask sb in

entrer dans un club/une firme   to join a club/firm

ça n'entre pas dans ce tiroir   it won't go into this drawer

40 envoyer

to send   *also* **renvoyer**
          to send back

PRESENT PARTICIPLE
envoyant

PAST PARTICIPLE
envoyé

PRESENT		IMPERFECT	
j'	envoie	j'	**envoy**ais
tu	envoies	tu	**envoy**ais
il	envoie	il	**envoy**ait
nous	**envoy**ons	nous	**envoy**ions
vous	**envoy**ez	vous	**envoy**iez
ils	envoient	ils	**envoy**aient

		FUTURE	
		j'	enverrai
		tu	enverras
		il	enverra
		nous	enverrons
		vous	enverrez
		ils	enverront

IMPERATIVE		CONDITIONAL	
	envoie	j'	enverrais
	envoyons	tu	enverrais
	envoyez	il	enverrait
		nous	enverrions
		vous	enverriez
		ils	enverraient

PAST HISTORIC		PRESENT SUBJUNCTIVE	
j'	**envoy**ai	j'	**envoie**
tu	**envoy**as	tu	**envoies**
il	**envoy**a	il	**envoie**
nous	**envoy**âmes	nous	**envoy**ions
vous	**envoy**âtes	vous	**envoy**iez
ils	**envoy**èrent	ils	**envoient**

PERFECT		PAST SUBJUNCTIVE	
j'	**ai envoy**é	j'	**envoy**asse
tu	**as envoy**é	tu	**envoy**asses
il	**a envoy**é	il	**envoy**ât
nous	**avons envoy**é	nous	**envoy**assions
vous	**avez envoy**é	vous	**envoy**assiez
ils	**ont envoy**é	ils	**envoy**assent

CONSTRUCTIONS
envoyer chercher qn/qch   to send for sb/sth

41 espérer
to hope

also **accélérer**
to accelerate

PRESENT PARTICIPLE
espérant

céder
to give up

PAST PARTICIPLE
espéré

compléter
to complete

PRESENT		*IMPERFECT*	
j'	**espère**	j'	**espérais**
tu	**espères**	tu	**espérais**
il	**espère**	il	**espérait**
nous	**espérons**	nous	**espérions**
vous	**espérez**	vous	**espériez**
ils	**espèrent**	ils	**espéraient**

		FUTURE	
		j'	**espérerai**
		tu	**espéreras**
		il	**espérera**
		nous	**espérerons**
		vous	**espérerez**
		ils	**espéreront**

IMPERATIVE		*CONDITIONAL*	
	espère	j'	**espérerais**
	espérons	tu	**espérerais**
	espérez	il	**espérerait**
		nous	**espérerions**
		vous	**espéreriez**
		ils	**espéreraient**

régler
to settle

sécher
to dry

PAST HISTORIC

j'	espérai
tu	espéras
il	espéra
nous	espérâmes
vous	espérâtes
ils	espérèrent

PERFECT

j'	ai espéré
tu	as espéré
il	a espéré
nous	avons espéré
vous	avez espéré
ils	ont espéré

PRESENT SUBJUNCTIVE

j'	espère
tu	espères
il	espère
nous	espérions
vous	espériez
ils	espèrent

PAST SUBJUNCTIVE

j'	espérasse
tu	espérasses
il	espérât
nous	espérassions
vous	espérassiez
ils	espérassent

CONSTRUCTIONS

espérer faire qch   to hope to do sth
viendra-t-il? – je l'espère (bien)   will he come? – I (certainly) hope so
j'espère bien n'avoir rien oublié   I hope I haven't forgotten anything

42 être
to be

PRESENT PARTICIPLE
étant

PAST PARTICIPLE
été

PRESENT		*IMPERFECT*	
je	suis	j'	étais
tu	es	tu	étais
il	est	il	était
nous	sommes	nous	étions
vous	êtes	vous	étiez
ils	sont	ils	étaient

		FUTURE	
		je	serai
		tu	seras
		il	sera
		nous	serons
		vous	serez
		ils	seront

IMPERATIVE		*CONDITIONAL*	
	sois	je	serais
	soyons	tu	serais
	soyez	il	serait
		nous	serions
		vous	seriez
		ils	seraient

PAST HISTORIC		PRESENT SUBJUNCTIVE	
je	fus	je	sois
tu	fus	tu	sois
il	fut	il	soit
nous	fûmes	nous	soyons
vous	fûtes	vous	soyez
ils	furent	ils	soient

PERFECT		PAST SUBJUNCTIVE	
j'	ai été	je	fusse
tu	as été	tu	fusses
il	a été	il	fût
nous	avons été	nous	fussions
vous	avez été	vous	fussiez
ils	ont été	ils	fussent

CONSTRUCTIONS

il est peintre   he's a painter

quel jour sommes-nous? – nous sommes le 12 mars
what's today's date? – it's March 12th

à qui est ce cahier? – il est à elle   whose jotter is this? –
it's hers

43 faire

to do; to make   *also* **contrefaire**
         to forge

PRESENT PARTICIPLE
faisant

défaire
   to undo

PAST PARTICIPLE
fait

refaire
   to redo

PRESENT

je	fais
tu	fais
il	fait
nous	faisons
vous	faites
ils	font

IMPERFECT

je	faisais
tu	faisais
il	faisait
nous	faisions
vous	faisiez
ils	faisaient

FUTURE

je	ferai
tu	feras
il	fera
nous	ferons
vous	ferez
ils	feront

IMPERATIVE

fais
faisons
faites

CONDITIONAL

je	ferais
tu	ferais
il	ferait
nous	ferions
vous	feriez
ils	feraient

satisfaire
to satisfy

PAST HISTORIC		PRESENT SUBJUNCTIVE	
je	fis	je	fasse
tu	fis	tu	fasses
il	fit	il	fasse
nous	fîmes	nous	fassions
vous	fîtes	vous	fassiez
ils	firent	ils	fassent
PERFECT		PAST SUBJUNCTIVE	
j'	ai fait	je	fisse
tu	as fait	tu	fisses
il	a fait	il	fît
nous	avons fait	nous	fissions
vous	avez fait	vous	fissiez
ils	ont fait	ils	fissent

CONSTRUCTIONS
faire la vaisselle/la cuisine   to do the dishes/the cooking
faire une promenade/des courses   to go for a walk/go shopping
il fait beau/du vent   it's nice/windy
faire faire qch   to have sth done *or* made

44 falloir
to be necessary

PRESENT PARTICIPLE
not used

PAST PARTICIPLE
fallu

PRESENT	IMPERFECT
il faut	**il fallait**
	FUTURE
	il faudra
IMPERATIVE	CONDITIONAL
not used	**il faudrait**

PAST HISTORIC **il fallut**	*PRESENT SUBJUNCTIVE* **il faille**
PERFECT **il a fallu**	*PAST SUBJUNCTIVE* **il fallût**

CONSTRUCTIONS

il lui faut quelqu'un pour l'aider   he needs somebody to help him

il faut qu'il parte   he'll have to *or* has to go

il faut être prudent   you have to be careful

45 finir
to finish   *also*   **agir**
           to act

PRESENT PARTICIPLE
finissant   **bâtir**
           to build

PAST PARTICIPLE
fini   **durcir**
           to harden

PRESENT		*IMPERFECT*	
je	**finis**	je	**finissais**
tu	**finis**	tu	**finissais**
il	**finit**	il	**finissait**
nous	**finissons**	nous	**finissions**
vous	**finissez**	vous	**finissiez**
ils	**finissent**	ils	**finissaient**

		FUTURE	
		je	**finirai**
		tu	**finiras**
		il	**finira**
		nous	**finirons**
		vous	**finirez**
		ils	**finiront**

IMPERATIVE		*CONDITIONAL*	
	finis	je	**finirais**
	finissons	tu	**finirais**
	finissez	il	**finirait**
		nous	**finirions**
		vous	**finiriez**
		ils	**finiraient**

guérir
  to heal

réunir
  to reunite

PAST HISTORIC		PRESENT SUBJUNCTIVE	
je	finis	je	finisse
tu	finis	tu	finisses
il	finit	il	finisse
nous	finîmes	nous	finissions
vous	finîtes	vous	finissiez
ils	finirent	ils	finissent

PERFECT		PAST SUBJUNCTIVE	
j'	ai fini	je	finisse
tu	as fini	tu	finisses
il	a fini	il	finît
nous	avons fini	nous	finissions
vous	avez fini	vous	finissiez
ils	ont fini	ils	finissent

CONSTRUCTIONS

finir de faire qch to finish doing sth
il a fini par comprendre he finally understood
tout finira par s'arranger everything will work out in the end
le film finit bien the film has a happy ending

46 fuir

to flee

also s'enfuir
to run away

PRESENT PARTICIPLE
fuyant

PAST PARTICIPLE
fui

PRESENT		IMPERFECT	
je	**fuis**	je	**fuyais**
tu	**fuis**	tu	**fuyais**
il	**fuit**	il	**fuyait**
nous	**fuyons**	nous	**fuyions**
vous	**fuyez**	vous	**fuyiez**
ils	**fuient**	ils	**fuyaient**

FUTURE
je	**fuirai**
tu	**fuiras**
il	**fuira**
nous	**fuirons**
vous	**fuirez**
ils	**fuiront**

IMPERATIVE
fuis
fuyons
fuyez

CONDITIONAL
je	**fuirais**
tu	**fuirais**
il	**fuirait**
nous	**fuirions**
vous	**fuiriez**
ils	**fuiraient**

PAST HISTORIC		PRESENT SUBJUNCTIVE	
je	**fuis**	je	**fuie**
tu	**fuis**	tu	**fuies**
il	**fuit**	il	**fuie**
nous	**fuîmes**	nous	**fuyions**
vous	**fuîtes**	vous	**fuyiez**
ils	**fuirent**	ils	**fuient**

PERFECT		PAST SUBJUNCTIVE	
j'	**ai** fui	je	**fuisse**
tu	**as** fui	tu	**fuisses**
il	**a** fui	il	**fuît**
nous	**avons** fui	nous	**fuissions**
vous	**avez** fui	vous	**fuissiez**
ils	**ont** fui	ils	**fuissent**

CONSTRUCTIONS
fuir devant un danger/ses responsabilités   to run away
from danger/one's responsibilities

47 haïr
to hate

PRESENT PARTICIPLE
haïssant

PAST PARTICIPLE
haï

PRESENT		*IMPERFECT*	
je	**hais**	je	**haïssais**
tu	**hais**	tu	**haïssais**
il	**hait**	il	**haïssait**
nous	**haïssons**	nous	**haïssions**
vous	**haïssez**	vous	**haïssiez**
ils	**haïssent**	ils	**haïssaient**

		FUTURE	
		je	**haïrai**
		tu	**haïras**
		il	**haïra**
		nous	**haïrons**
		vous	**haïrez**
		ils	**haïront**

IMPERATIVE		*CONDITIONAL*	
	hais	je	**haïrais**
	haïssons	tu	**haïrais**
	haïssez	il	**haïrait**
		nous	**haïrions**
		vous	**haïriez**
		ils	**haïraient**

PAST HISTORIC		PRESENT SUBJUNCTIVE	
je	**haïs**	je	**haïsse**
tu	**haïs**	tu	**haïsses**
il	**haït**	il	**haïsse**
nous	**haïmes**	nous	**haïssions**
vous	**haïtes**	vous	**haïssiez**
ils	**haïrent**	ils	**haïssent**

PERFECT		PAST SUBJUNCTIVE	
j'	**ai** haï	je	**haïsse**
tu	**as** haï	tu	**haïsses**
il	**a** haï	il	**haït**
nous	**avons** haï	nous	**haïssions**
vous	**avez** haï	vous	**haïssiez**
ils	**ont** haï	ils	**haïssent**

48 interdire
to forbid *also* **contredire**
to contradict

PRESENT PARTICIPLE
interdisant

prédire
to predict

PAST PARTICIPLE
interdit

PRESENT
j'	**interdis**
tu	**interdis**
il	**interdit**
nous	**interdisons**
vous	**interdisez**
ils	**interdisent**

IMPERFECT
j'	**interdisais**
tu	**interdisais**
il	**interdisait**
nous	**interdisions**
vous	**interdisiez**
ils	**interdisaient**

FUTURE
j'	**interdirai**
tu	**interdiras**
il	**interdira**
nous	**interdirons**
vous	**interdirez**
ils	**interdiront**

IMPERATIVE
interdis
interdisons
interdisez

CONDITIONAL
j'	**interdirais**
tu	**interdirais**
il	**interdirait**
nous	**interdirions**
vous	**interdiriez**
ils	**interdiraient**

to forbid

PAST HISTORIC		PRESENT SUBJUNCTIVE	
j'	interdis	j'	interdise
tu	interdis	tu	interdises
il	interdit	il	interdise
nous	interdîmes	nous	interdisions
vous	interdîtes	vous	interdisiez
ils	interdirent	ils	interdisent

PERFECT		PAST SUBJUNCTIVE	
j'	ai interdit	j'	interdisse
tu	as interdit	tu	interdisses
il	a interdit	il	interdît
nous	avons interdit	nous	interdissions
vous	avez interdit	vous	interdissiez
ils	ont interdit	ils	interdissent

CONSTRUCTIONS

interdire à qn de faire qch   to forbid sb to do sth
il m'a interdit l'alcool/le tabac   he's forbidden me to
drink/smoke
il est interdit de fumer   smoking is prohibited
stationnement interdit   no parking

49 introduire
to introduce

PRESENT PARTICIPLE
introduisant

PAST PARTICIPLE
introduit

PRESENT

j'	**introduis**
tu	**introduis**
il	**introduit**
nous	**introduisons**
vous	**introduisez**
ils	**introduisent**

IMPERFECT

j'	**introduisais**
tu	**introduisais**
il	**introduisait**
nous	**introduisions**
vous	**introduisiez**
ils	**introduisaient**

FUTURE

j'	**introduirai**
tu	**introduiras**
il	**introduira**
nous	**introduirons**
vous	**introduirez**
ils	**introduiront**

IMPERATIVE

introduis
introduisons
introduisez

CONDITIONAL

j'	**introduirais**
tu	**introduirais**
il	**introduirait**
nous	**introduirions**
vous	**introduiriez**
ils	**introduiraient**

to introduce

PAST HISTORIC		PRESENT SUBJUNCTIVE	
j'	introduisis	j'	introduise
tu	introduisis	tu	introduises
il	introduisit	il	introduise
nous	introduisîmes	nous	introduisions
vous	introduisîtes	vous	introduisiez
ils	introduisirent	ils	introduisent

PERFECT		PAST SUBJUNCTIVE	
j'	ai introduit	j'	introduisisse
tu	as introduit	tu	introduisisses
il	a introduit	il	introduisît
nous	avons introduit	nous	introduisissions
vous	avez introduit	vous	introduisissiez
ils	ont introduit	ils	introduisissent

CONSTRUCTIONS

il a introduit sa clef dans la serrure he inserted his key in the lock

il m'a introduit dans le salon he showed me into the lounge

s'introduire dans une pièce to get into a room

50 jeter

to throw

also **breveter**
to patent

PRESENT PARTICIPLE
jetant

étiqueter
to label

PAST PARTICIPLE
jeté

feuilleter
to leaf through

PRESENT		IMPERFECT	
je	**jette**	je	**jetais**
tu	**jettes**	tu	**jetais**
il	**jette**	il	**jetait**
nous	**jetons**	nous	**jetions**
vous	**jetez**	vous	**jetiez**
ils	**jettent**	ils	**jetaient**

		FUTURE	
		je	**jetterai**
		tu	**jetteras**
		il	**jettera**
		nous	**jetterons**
		vous	**jetterez**
		ils	**jetteront**

IMPERATIVE	CONDITIONAL	
jette	je	**jetterais**
jetons	tu	**jetterais**
jetez	il	**jetterait**
	nous	**jetterions**
	vous	**jetteriez**
	ils	**jetteraient**

projeter
to plan

rejeter
to reject

PAST HISTORIC

je	**jet**ai
tu	**jet**as
il	**jet**a
nous	**jet**âmes
vous	**jet**âtes
ils	**jet**èrent

PRESENT SUBJUNCTIVE

je	**jet**te
tu	**jet**tes
il	**jet**te
nous	**jet**ions
vous	**jet**iez
ils	**jet**tent

PERFECT

j'	**ai jet**é
tu	**as jet**é
il	**a jet**é
nous	**avons jet**é
vous	**avez jet**é
ils	**ont jet**é

PAST SUBJUNCTIVE

je	**jet**asse
tu	**jet**asses
il	**jet**ât
nous	**jet**assions
vous	**jet**assiez
ils	**jet**assent

CONSTRUCTIONS

jeter qch à qn   to throw sth to sb; to throw sth at sb
jeter qch par terre/par la fenêtre   to throw sth down/out
of the window
jeter qn dehors *or* **à la porte**   to throw sb out

51 joindre

to join   *also* **adjoindre**
             to attach

PRESENT PARTICIPLE
joignant   **rejoindre**
             to rejoin

PAST PARTICIPLE
joint

PRESENT		IMPERFECT	
je	joins	je	joignais
tu	joins	tu	joignais
il	joint	il	joignait
nous	joignons	nous	joignions
vous	joignez	vous	joigniez
ils	joignent	ils	joignaient

		FUTURE	
		je	joindrai
		tu	joindras
		il	joindra
		nous	joindrons
		vous	joindrez
		ils	joindront

IMPERATIVE	CONDITIONAL	
joins	je	joindrais
joignons	tu	joindrais
joignez	il	joindrait
	nous	joindrions
	vous	joindriez
	ils	joindraient

PAST HISTORIC		PRESENT SUBJUNCTIVE	
je	joignis	je	joigne
tu	joignis	tu	joignes
il	joignit	il	joigne
nous	joignîmes	nous	joignions
vous	joignîtes	vous	joigniez
ils	joignirent	ils	joignent

PERFECT			PAST SUBJUNCTIVE	
j'	ai	joint	je	joignisse
tu	as	joint	tu	joignisses
il	a	joint	il	joignît
nous	avons	joint	nous	joignissions
vous	avez	joint	vous	joignissiez
ils	ont	joint	ils	joignissent

CONSTRUCTIONS

joindre les mains to clasp one's hands (together)
voir la lettre ci-jointe see the enclosed letter
elle joint l'intelligence à la beauté she combines
intelligence and beauty
se joindre à to join

52 lever

to lift   *also*   amener
                         to bring

PRESENT PARTICIPLE
levant   élever
                         to raise

PAST PARTICIPLE
levé   enlever
                         to remove

PRESENT		IMPERFECT	
je	**lè**ve	je	**lev**ais
tu	**lè**ves	tu	**lev**ais
il	**lè**ve	il	**lev**ait
nous	**lev**ons	nous	**lev**ions
vous	**lev**ez	vous	**lev**iez
ils	**lè**vent	ils	**lev**aient

FUTURE	
je	**lè**verai
tu	**lè**veras
il	**lè**vera
nous	**lè**verons
vous	**lè**verez
ils	**lè**veront

IMPERATIVE	CONDITIONAL	
lève	je	**lè**verais
levons	tu	**lè**verais
levez	il	**lè**verait
	nous	**lè**verions
	vous	**lè**veriez
	ils	**lè**veraient

mener
to lead

peser
to weigh

to lift

PAST HISTORIC
je	**levai**
tu	**levas**
il	**leva**
nous	**levâmes**
vous	**levâtes**
ils	**levèrent**

PERFECT
j'	**ai levé**
tu	**as levé**
il	**a levé**
nous	**avons levé**
vous	**avez levé**
ils	**ont levé**

PRESENT SUBJUNCTIVE
je	**lève**
tu	**lèves**
il	**lève**
nous	**levions**
vous	**leviez**
ils	**lèvent**

PAST SUBJUNCTIVE
je	**levasse**
tu	**levasses**
il	**levât**
nous	**levassions**
vous	**levassiez**
ils	**levassent**

CONSTRUCTIONS
lever les yeux to look up
levez la main! put your hand up!
lever son verre à qn to raise one's glass to sb
se lever to get up; to rise
le jour/la brume se lève day breaks/the mist is clearing

53 lire

to read   *also* **élire**

                                  to elect

PRESENT PARTICIPLE
lisant

PAST PARTICIPLE
lu

PRESENT		*IMPERFECT*	
je	**lis**	je	**lisais**
tu	**lis**	tu	**lisais**
il	**lit**	il	**lisait**
nous	**lisons**	nous	**lisions**
vous	**lisez**	vous	**lisiez**
ils	**lisent**	ils	**lisaient**

		FUTURE	
		je	**lirai**
		tu	**liras**
		il	**lira**
		nous	**lirons**
		vous	**lirez**
		ils	**liront**

IMPERATIVE		*CONDITIONAL*	
	lis	je	**lirais**
	lisons	tu	**lirais**
	lisez	il	**lirait**
		nous	**lirions**
		vous	**liriez**
		ils	**liraient**

PAST HISTORIC	PRESENT SUBJUNCTIVE
je **lus**	je **lise**
tu **lus**	tu **lises**
il **lut**	il **lise**
nous **lûmes**	nous **lisions**
vous **lûtes**	vous **lisiez**
ils **lurent**	ils **lisent**
PERFECT	PAST SUBJUNCTIVE
j' **ai lu**	je **lusse**
tu **as lu**	tu **lusses**
il **a lu**	il **lût**
nous **avons lu**	nous **lussions**
vous **avez lu**	vous **lussiez**
ils **ont lu**	ils **lussent**

CONSTRUCTIONS

je lui ai lu une histoire   I read him a story
c'est un livre à lire   it's a book you should read

54 manger
to eat

also **arranger**
to arrange

PRESENT PARTICIPLE
mangeant

bouger
to move

PAST PARTICIPLE
mangé

dégager
to clear

PRESENT
je	**mang**e
tu	**mang**es
il	**mang**e
nous	**mang**eons
vous	**mang**ez
ils	**mang**ent

IMPERFECT
je	**mang**eais
tu	**mang**eais
il	**mang**eait
nous	**mang**ions
vous	**mang**iez
ils	**mang**eaient

FUTURE
je	**mang**erai
tu	**mang**eras
il	**mang**era
nous	**mang**erons
vous	**mang**erez
ils	**mang**eront

IMPERATIVE
mange
mangeons
mangez

CONDITIONAL
je	**mang**erais
tu	**mang**erais
il	**mang**erait
nous	**mang**erions
vous	**mang**eriez
ils	**mang**eraient

to eat

diriger
  to manage

loger
  to accommodate

PAST HISTORIC		PRESENT SUBJUNCTIVE	
je	mangeai	je	mange
tu	mangeas	tu	manges
il	mangea	il	mange
nous	mangeâmes	nous	mangions
vous	mangeâtes	vous	mangiez
ils	mangèrent	ils	mangent

PERFECT		PAST SUBJUNCTIVE	
j'	ai mangé	je	mangeasse
tu	as mangé	tu	mangeasses
il	a mangé	il	mangeât
nous	avons mangé	nous	mangeassions
vous	avez mangé	vous	mangeassiez
ils	ont mangé	ils	mangeassent

CONSTRUCTIONS
manger comme quatre   to eat like a horse
est-ce que ça se mange?   is it edible?

55 maudire
to curse

PRESENT PARTICIPLE
maudissant

PAST PARTICIPLE
maudit

PRESENT
je	**maudis**
tu	**maudis**
il	**maudit**
nous	**maudissons**
vous	**maudissez**
ils	**maudissent**

IMPERFECT
je	**maudissais**
tu	**maudissais**
il	**maudissait**
nous	**maudissions**
vous	**maudissiez**
ils	**maudissaient**

FUTURE
je	**maudirai**
tu	**maudiras**
il	**maudira**
nous	**maudirons**
vous	**maudirez**
ils	**maudiront**

IMPERATIVE
maudis
maudissons
maudissez

CONDITIONAL
je	**maudirais**
tu	**maudirais**
il	**maudirait**
nous	**maudirions**
vous	**maudiriez**
ils	**maudiraient**

to curse

PAST HISTORIC		*PRESENT SUBJUNCTIVE*	
je	maudis	je	maudisse
tu	maudis	tu	maudisses
il	maudit	il	maudisse
nous	maudîmes	nous	maudissions
vous	maudîtes	vous	maudissiez
ils	maudirent	ils	maudissent

PERFECT		*PAST SUBJUNCTIVE*	
j'	**ai** maudit	je	maudisse
tu	**as** maudit	tu	maudisses
il	**a** maudit	il	maudît
nous	**avons** maudit	nous	maudissions
vous	**avez** maudit	vous	maudissiez
ils	**ont** maudit	ils	maudissent

CONSTRUCTIONS

ce maudit stylo ne marche pas!   this blasted pen won't work!

56 mettre
to put

also **admettre**
to admit

commettre
to commit

émettre
to emit

PRESENT PARTICIPLE
mettant

PAST PARTICIPLE
mis

PRESENT		*IMPERFECT*	
je	**mets**	je	**mettais**
tu	**mets**	tu	**mettais**
il	**met**	il	**mettait**
nous	**mettons**	nous	**mettions**
vous	**mettez**	vous	**mettiez**
ils	**mettent**	ils	**mettaient**

		FUTURE	
		je	**mettrai**
		tu	**mettras**
		il	**mettra**
		nous	**mettrons**
		vous	**mettrez**
		ils	**mettront**

IMPERATIVE	*CONDITIONAL*	
mets	je	**mettrais**
mettons	tu	**mettrais**
mettez	il	**mettrait**
	nous	**mettrions**
	vous	**mettriez**
	ils	**mettraient**

soumettre
to submit

transmettre
to transmit

PAST HISTORIC		PRESENT SUBJUNCTIVE	
je	mis	je	**mette**
tu	mis	tu	**mettes**
il	mit	il	**mette**
nous	mîmes	nous	**mettions**
vous	mîtes	vous	**mettiez**
ils	mirent	ils	**mettent**

PERFECT		PAST SUBJUNCTIVE	
j'	**ai** mis	je	misse
tu	**as** mis	tu	misses
il	**a** mis	il	mît
nous	**avons** mis	nous	missions
vous	**avez** mis	vous	missiez
ils	**ont** mis	ils	missent

CONSTRUCTIONS

j'ai mis 2 heures à le faire   I took 2 hours to do it
elle n'a rien à se mettre   she's nothing to wear
se mettre à faire qch   to start doing sth
se mettre au travail   to set to work

57 monter
to go up

PRESENT PARTICIPLE
montant

PAST PARTICIPLE
monté

PRESENT		IMPERFECT	
je	**mont**e	je	**mont**ais
tu	**mont**es	tu	**mont**ais
il	**mont**e	il	**mont**ait
nous	**mont**ons	nous	**mont**ions
vous	**mont**ez	vous	**mont**iez
ils	**mont**ent	ils	**mont**aient

		FUTURE	
		je	**mont**erai
		tu	**mont**eras
		il	**mont**era
		nous	**mont**erons
		vous	**mont**erez
		ils	**mont**eront

IMPERATIVE	CONDITIONAL	
monte	je	**mont**erais
montons	tu	**mont**erais
montez	il	**mont**erait
	nous	**mont**erions
	vous	**mont**eriez
	ils	**mont**eraient

to go up

PAST HISTORIC		PRESENT SUBJUNCTIVE	
je	montai	je	monte
tu	montas	tu	montes
il	monta	il	monte
nous	montâmes	nous	montions
vous	montâtes	vous	montiez
ils	montèrent	ils	montent

PERFECT		PAST SUBJUNCTIVE	
je	suis monté	je	montasse
tu	es monté	tu	montasses
il	est monté	il	montât
nous	sommes montés	nous	montassions
vous	êtes monté(s)	vous	montassiez
ils	sont montés	ils	montassent

CONSTRUCTIONS

monter dans un train/un avion   to get on a train/plane
monter en voiture   to get into a car
monter à bicyclette/cheval   to get on a bicycle/horse; to ride a bicycle/horse
il a monté la valise   he took the case up

58 mordre
to bite   *also* **tordre**
to twist

PRESENT PARTICIPLE
mordant

PAST PARTICIPLE
mordu

PRESENT
je	**mords**
tu	**mords**
il	**mord**
nous	**mordons**
vous	**mordez**
ils	**mordent**

IMPERFECT
je	**mordais**
tu	**mordais**
il	**mordait**
nous	**mordions**
vous	**mordiez**
ils	**mordaient**

FUTURE
je	**mordrai**
tu	**mordras**
il	**mordra**
nous	**mordrons**
vous	**mordrez**
ils	**mordront**

IMPERATIVE
mords
mordons
mordez

CONDITIONAL
je	**mordrais**
tu	**mordrais**
il	**mordrait**
nous	**mordrions**
vous	**mordriez**
ils	**mordraient**

PAST HISTORIC		PRESENT SUBJUNCTIVE	
je	mordis	je	morde
tu	mordis	tu	mordes
il	mordit	il	morde
nous	mordîmes	nous	mordions
vous	mordîtes	vous	mordiez
ils	mordirent	ils	mordent

PERFECT		PAST SUBJUNCTIVE	
j'	ai mordu	je	mordisse
tu	as mordu	tu	mordisses
il	a mordu	il	mordît
nous	avons mordu	nous	mordissions
vous	avez mordu	vous	mordissiez
ils	ont mordu	ils	mordissent

CONSTRUCTIONS

mordre qn à la main to bite sb's hand
mordre dans une pomme to bite into an apple
mordu de football mad keen on football
mordre à l'hameçon to rise to the bait

59 moudre
to grind

PRESENT PARTICIPLE
moulant

PAST PARTICIPLE
moulu

PRESENT
je	**mouds**
tu	**mouds**
il	**moud**
nous	**moulons**
vous	**moulez**
ils	**moulent**

IMPERFECT
je	**moulais**
tu	**moulais**
il	**moulait**
nous	**moulions**
vous	**mouliez**
ils	**moulaient**

FUTURE
je	**moudrai**
tu	**moudras**
il	**moudra**
nous	**moudrons**
vous	**moudrez**
ils	**moudront**

IMPERATIVE
mouds
moulons
moulez

CONDITIONAL
je	**moudrais**
tu	**moudrais**
il	**moudrait**
nous	**moudrions**
vous	**moudriez**
ils	**moudraient**

PAST HISTORIC		PRESENT SUBJUNCTIVE	
je	moulus	je	moule
tu	moulus	tu	moules
il	moulut	il	moule
nous	moulûmes	nous	moulions
vous	moulûtes	vous	mouliez
ils	moulurent	ils	moulent

PERFECT		PAST SUBJUNCTIVE	
j'	ai moulu	je	moulusse
tu	as moulu	tu	moulusses
il	a moulu	il	moulût
nous	avons moulu	nous	moulussions
vous	avez moulu	vous	moulussiez
ils	ont moulu	ils	moulussent

CONSTRUCTIONS

je l'aimerais moulu très fin, s'il vous plaît I'd like it very finely ground, please

60 mourir
to die

PRESENT PARTICIPLE
mourant

PAST PARTICIPLE
mort

PRESENT

je	**meurs**
tu	**meurs**
il	**meurt**
nous	**mourons**
vous	**mourez**
ils	**meurent**

IMPERFECT

je	**mourais**
tu	**mourais**
il	**mourait**
nous	**mourions**
vous	**mouriez**
ils	**mouraient**

FUTURE

je	**mourrai**
tu	**mourras**
il	**mourra**
nous	**mourrons**
vous	**mourrez**
ils	**mourront**

IMPERATIVE

meurs
mourons
mourez

CONDITIONAL

je	**mourrais**
tu	**mourrais**
il	**mourrait**
nous	**mourrions**
vous	**mourriez**
ils	**mourraient**

PAST HISTORIC		PRESENT SUBJUNCTIVE	
je	**mourus**	je	**meure**
tu	**mourus**	tu	**meures**
il	**mourut**	il	**meure**
nous	**mourûmes**	nous	**mourions**
vous	**mourûtes**	vous	**mouriez**
ils	**moururent**	ils	**meurent**

PERFECT		PAST SUBJUNCTIVE	
je	**suis mort**	je	**mourusse**
tu	**es mort**	tu	**mourusses**
il	**est mort**	il	**mourût**
nous	**sommes mort**	nous	**mourussions**
vous	**êtes mort(s)**	vous	**mourussiez**
ils	**sont morts**	ils	**mourussent**

CONSTRUCTIONS
il est mort he's dead
il est mort en 1960 he died in 1960
mourir de faim/froid to die of hunger/cold
être mort de peur to be scared to death
mourir d'envie de faire qch to be dying to do sth

61 mouvoir
to move

PRESENT PARTICIPLE
mouvant

PAST PARTICIPLE
mû (*NB*: **mue, mus, mues**)

PRESENT		*IMPERFECT*	
je	**meus**	je	**mouvais**
tu	**meus**	tu	**mouvais**
il	**meut**	il	**mouvait**
nous	**mouvons**	nous	**mouvions**
vous	**mouvez**	vous	**mouviez**
ils	**meuvent**	ils	**mouvaient**

		FUTURE	
		je	**mouvrai**
		tu	**mouvras**
		il	**mouvra**
		nous	**mouvrons**
		vous	**mouvrez**
		ils	**mouvront**

IMPERATIVE		*CONDITIONAL*	
	meus	je	**mouvrais**
	mouvons	tu	**mouvrais**
	mouvez	il	**mouvrait**
		nous	**mouvrions**
		vous	**mouvriez**
		ils	**mouvraient**

PAST HISTORIC		*PRESENT SUBJUNCTIVE*	
je	mus	je	meuve
tu	mus	tu	meuves
il	mut	il	meuve
nous	mûmes	nous	mouvions
vous	mûtes	vous	mouviez
ils	murent	ils	meuvent

PERFECT		*PAST SUBJUNCTIVE*	
j'	ai mû	je	musse
tu	as mû	tu	musses
il	a mû	il	mût
nous	avons mû	nous	mussions
vous	avez mû	vous	mussiez
ils	ont mû	ils	mussent

CONSTRUCTIONS

il a de la peine à se mouvoir   he has difficulty in moving

62 naître

to be born

PRESENT PARTICIPLE
naissant

PAST PARTICIPLE
né

PRESENT		*IMPERFECT*	
je	**nais**	je	**naissais**
tu	**nais**	tu	**naissais**
il	**naît**	il	**naissait**
nous	**naissons**	nous	**naissions**
vous	**naissez**	vous	**naissiez**
ils	**naissent**	ils	**naissaient**

		FUTURE	
		je	**naîtrai**
		tu	**naîtras**
		il	**naîtra**
		nous	**naîtrons**
		vous	**naîtrez**
		ils	**naîtront**

IMPERATIVE	*CONDITIONAL*	
nais	je	**naîtrais**
naissons	tu	**naîtrais**
naissez	il	**naîtrait**
	nous	**naîtrions**
	vous	**naîtriez**
	ils	**naîtraient**

naître 62

to be born

PAST HISTORIC

je	naquis
tu	naquis
il	naquit
nous	naquîmes
vous	naquîtes
ils	naquirent

PERFECT

je	suis né
tu	es né
il	est né
nous	sommes nés
vous	êtes né(s)
ils	sont nés

PRESENT SUBJUNCTIVE

je	naisse
tu	naisses
il	naisse
nous	naissions
vous	naissiez
ils	naissent

PAST SUBJUNCTIVE

je	naquisse
tu	naquisses
il	naquît
nous	naquissions
vous	naquissiez
ils	naquissent

CONSTRUCTIONS

je suis né le 5 mars I was born on 5th March
il naît plus de filles que de garçons there are more girls born than boys
faire naître des soupçons to arouse suspicion

63 nettoyer
to clean

also **aboyer**
to bark

PRESENT PARTICIPLE
nettoyant

appuyer
to lean

PAST PARTICIPLE
nettoyé

employer
to use

PRESENT
je	nettoie
tu	nettoies
il	nettoie
nous	nettoyons
vous	nettoyez
ils	nettoient

IMPERFECT
je	nettoyais
tu	nettoyais
il	nettoyait
nous	nettoyions
vous	nettoyiez
ils	nettoyaient

FUTURE
je	nettoierai
tu	nettoieras
il	nettoiera
nous	nettoierons
vous	nettoierez
ils	nettoieront

IMPERATIVE
nettoie
nettoyons
nettoyez

CONDITIONAL
je	nettoierais
tu	nettoierais
il	nettoierait
nous	nettoierions
vous	nettoieriez
ils	nettoieraient

to clean

ennuyer
to bore

essuyer
to wipe

PAST HISTORIC		*PRESENT SUBJUNCTIVE*	
je	**nettoyai**	je	**nettoie**
tu	**nettoyas**	tu	**nettoies**
il	**nettoya**	il	**nettoie**
nous	**nettoyâmes**	nous	**nettoyions**
vous	**nettoyâtes**	vous	**nettoyiez**
ils	**nettoyèrent**	ils	**nettoient**

PERFECT		*PAST SUBJUNCTIVE*	
j'	**ai nettoyé**	je	**nettoyasse**
tu	**as nettoyé**	tu	**nettoyasses**
il	**a nettoyé**	il	**nettoyât**
nous	**avons nettoyé**	nous	**nettoyassions**
vous	**avez nettoyé**	vous	**nettoyassiez**
ils	**ont nettoyé**	ils	**nettoyassent**

CONSTRUCTIONS
nettoyer à sec to dry-clean

64 obtenir
to get

PRESENT PARTICIPLE
obtenant

PAST PARTICIPLE
obtenu

	PRESENT		*IMPERFECT*
j'	obtiens	j'	**obten**ais
tu	obtiens	tu	**obten**ais
il	obtient	il	**obten**ait
nous	**obten**ons	nous	**obten**ions
vous	**obten**ez	vous	**obten**iez
ils	obtiennent	ils	**obten**aient

	FUTURE
j'	**obtiendr**ai
tu	**obtiendr**as
il	**obtiendr**a
nous	**obtiendr**ons
vous	**obtiendr**ez
ils	**obtiendr**ont

	IMPERATIVE		*CONDITIONAL*
	obtiens	j'	**obtiendr**ais
	obtenons	tu	**obtiendr**ais
	obtenez	il	**obtiendr**ait
		nous	**obtiendr**ions
		vous	**obtiendr**iez
		ils	**obtiendr**aient

PAST HISTORIC		PRESENT SUBJUNCTIVE	
j'	obtins	j'	obtienne
tu	obtins	tu	obtiennes
il	obtint	il	obtienne
nous	obtînmes	nous	obtenions
vous	obtîntes	vous	obteniez
ils	obtinrent	ils	obtiennent
PERFECT		PAST SUBJUNCTIVE	
j'	ai obtenu	j'	obtinsse
tu	as obtenu	tu	obtinsses
il	a obtenu	il	obtînt
nous	avons obtenu	nous	obtinssions
vous	avez obtenu	vous	obtinssiez
ils	ont obtenu	ils	obtinssent

CONSTRUCTIONS

obtenir qch de qn   to get sth from sb
obtenir de qn qu'il fasse qch   to get sb to do sth

65 offrir

to offer   *also* **souffrir**
         to suffer

PRESENT PARTICIPLE
offrant

PAST PARTICIPLE
offert

	PRESENT		*IMPERFECT*
j'	**offre**	j'	**offrais**
tu	**offres**	tu	**offrais**
il	**offre**	il	**offrait**
nous	**offrons**	nous	**offrions**
vous	**offrez**	vous	**offriez**
ils	**offrent**	ils	**offraient**

FUTURE

j'	**offrirai**
tu	**offriras**
il	**offrira**
nous	**offrirons**
vous	**offrirez**
ils	**offriront**

IMPERATIVE

offre
offrons
offrez

CONDITIONAL

j'	**offrirais**
tu	**offrirais**
il	**offrirait**
nous	**offririons**
vous	**offririez**
ils	**offriraient**

PAST HISTORIC		PRESENT SUBJUNCTIVE	
j'	**offris**	j'	**offre**
tu	**offris**	tu	**offres**
il	**offrit**	il	**offre**
nous	**offrîmes**	nous	**offrions**
vous	**offrîtes**	vous	**offriez**
ils	**offrirent**	ils	**offrent**

PERFECT		PAST SUBJUNCTIVE	
j'	**ai** offert	j'	**offrisse**
tu	**as** offert	tu	**offrisses**
il	**a** offert	il	**offrît**
nous	**avons** offert	nous	**offrissions**
vous	**avez** offert	vous	**offrissiez**
ils	**ont** offert	ils	**offrissent**

CONSTRUCTIONS

offrir qch à qn   to give sb sth; to offer sb sth
offrir de faire qch   to offer to do sth
s'offrir un bon repas/un disque   to treat oneself to a good meal/a record
il s'est offert en otage/comme guide   he volunteered to be *or* as a hostage/guide

66 ouvrir

to open   *also*   **rouvrir**
                          to reopen

PRESENT PARTICIPLE
ouvrant

PAST PARTICIPLE
ouvert

PRESENT

j'	**ouvre**
tu	**ouvres**
il	**ouvre**
nous	**ouvrons**
vous	**ouvrez**
ils	**ouvrent**

IMPERFECT

j'	**ouvr**ais
tu	**ouvr**ais
il	**ouvr**ait
nous	**ouvr**ions
vous	**ouvr**iez
ils	**ouvr**aient

FUTURE

j'	**ouvrir**ai
tu	**ouvrir**as
il	**ouvrir**a
nous	**ouvrir**ons
vous	**ouvrir**ez
ils	**ouvrir**ont

IMPERATIVE

ouvre
ouvrons
ouvrez

CONDITIONAL

j'	**ouvrir**ais
tu	**ouvrir**ais
il	**ouvrir**ait
nous	**ouvrir**ions
vous	**ouvrir**iez
ils	**ouvrir**aient

PAST HISTORIC		PRESENT SUBJUNCTIVE	
j'	**ouvris**	j'	**ouvre**
tu	**ouvris**	tu	**ouvres**
il	**ouvrit**	il	**ouvre**
nous	**ouvrîmes**	nous	**ouvrions**
vous	**ouvrîtes**	vous	**ouvriez**
ils	**ouvrirent**	ils	**ouvrent**

PERFECT		PAST SUBJUNCTIVE	
j'	**ai** ouvert	j'	**ouvrisse**
tu	**as** ouvert	tu	**ouvrisses**
il	**a** ouvert	il	**ouvrît**
nous	**avons** ouvert	nous	**ouvrissions**
vous	**avez** ouvert	vous	**ouvrissiez**
ils	**ont** ouvert	ils	**ouvrissent**

CONSTRUCTIONS

ouvrir une porte toute grande   to open a door wide
ouvrir l'électricité/le gaz/la radio   to switch *or* turn on
the electricity/gas/radio
notre épicier ouvre le lundi   our grocer is open on
Mondays
s'ouvrir   to open; to open up; to open out

67 paraître

to appear *also* **disparaître**
to disappear

PRESENT PARTICIPLE
paraissant

PAST PARTICIPLE
paru

PRESENT
je	**parais**
tu	**parais**
il	**paraît**
nous	**paraissons**
vous	**paraissez**
ils	**paraissent**

IMPERFECT
je	**paraissais**
tu	**paraissais**
il	**paraissait**
nous	**paraissions**
vous	**paraissiez**
ils	**paraissaient**

FUTURE
je	**paraîtrai**
tu	**paraîtras**
il	**paraîtra**
nous	**paraîtrons**
vous	**paraîtrez**
ils	**paraîtront**

IMPERATIVE
parais
paraissons
paraissez

CONDITIONAL
je	**paraîtrais**
tu	**paraîtrais**
il	**paraîtrait**
nous	**paraîtrions**
vous	**paraîtriez**
ils	**paraîtraient**

PAST HISTORIC		PRESENT SUBJUNCTIVE	
je	**parus**	je	**paraisse**
tu	**parus**	tu	**paraisses**
il	**parut**	il	**paraisse**
nous	**parûmes**	nous	**paraissions**
vous	**parûtes**	vous	**paraissiez**
ils	**parurent**	ils	**paraissent**

PERFECT		PAST SUBJUNCTIVE	
j'	**ai paru**	je	**parusse**
tu	**as paru**	tu	**parusses**
il	**a paru**	il	**parût**
nous	**avons paru**	nous	**parussions**
vous	**avez paru**	vous	**parussiez**
ils	**ont paru**	ils	**parussent**

CONSTRUCTIONS

paraître faire qch   to seem to do sth

'vient de paraître' 'just out'

'à paraître prochainement' 'out soon'

il est malade, paraît-il,   il paraît qu'il est malade   he's ill apparently

68 partir

to go, leave

PRESENT PARTICIPLE
partant

PAST PARTICIPLE
parti

PRESENT		IMPERFECT	
je	**pars**	je	**partais**
tu	**pars**	tu	**partais**
il	**part**	il	**partait**
nous	**partons**	nous	**partions**
vous	**partez**	vous	**partiez**
ils	**partent**	ils	**partaient**

		FUTURE	
		je	**partirai**
		tu	**partiras**
		il	**partira**
		nous	**partirons**
		vous	**partirez**
		ils	**partiront**

IMPERATIVE	CONDITIONAL	
pars	je	**partirais**
partons	tu	**partirais**
partez	il	**partirait**
	nous	**partirions**
	vous	**partiriez**
	ils	**partiraient**

PAST HISTORIC		PRESENT SUBJUNCTIVE	
je	partis	je	parte
tu	partis	tu	partes
il	partit	il	parte
nous	partîmes	nous	partions
vous	partîtes	vous	partiez
ils	partirent	ils	partent

PERFECT		PAST SUBJUNCTIVE	
je	suis parti	je	partisse
tu	es parti	tu	partisses
il	est parti	il	partît
nous	sommes partis	nous	partissions
vous	êtes parti(s)	vous	partissiez
ils	sont partis	ils	partissent

CONSTRUCTIONS

partir en vacances/en voyage   to go (off) on holiday/on a journey

à partir du 14 juillet   as from the 14th of July

à partir de 100 F   from 100 F upwards

69 passer

to pass · *also* **dépasser**
to overtake

PRESENT PARTICIPLE
passant

surpasser
to surpass

PAST PARTICIPLE
passé

PRESENT
je	passe
tu	passes
il	passe
nous	passons
vous	passez
ils	passent

IMPERFECT
je	passais
tu	passais
il	passait
nous	passions
vous	passiez
ils	passaient

FUTURE
je	passerai
tu	passeras
il	passera
nous	passerons
vous	passerez
ils	passeront

IMPERATIVE
passe
passons
passez

CONDITIONAL
je	passerais
tu	passerais
il	passerait
nous	passerions
vous	passeriez
ils	passeraient

PAST HISTORIC		PRESENT SUBJUNCTIVE	
je	**passai**	je	**passe**
tu	**passas**	tu	**passes**
il	**passa**	il	**passe**
nous	**passâmes**	nous	**passions**
vous	**passâtes**	vous	**passiez**
ils	**passèrent**	ils	**passent**

PERFECT		PAST SUBJUNCTIVE	
j'	**ai passé**	je	**passasse**
tu	**as passé**	tu	**passasses**
il	**a passé**	il	**passât**
nous	**avons passé**	nous	**passassions**
vous	**avez passé**	vous	**passassiez**
ils	**ont passé**	ils	**passassent**

CONSTRUCTIONS

passer en courant   to run past
passer au bureau/chez un ami   to call (in) at the office/at a friend's
laisser passer qn   to let sb through *or* in *etc*
laisser passer une erreur   to overlook a mistake
passer un examen   to sit an exam

70 payer

to pay

also **balayer**
to sweep up

PRESENT PARTICIPLE
payant

débrayer
to declutch

PAST PARTICIPLE
payé

délayer
to thin down

PRESENT
je	**pay**e
tu	**pay**es
il	**pay**e
nous	**pay**ons
vous	**pay**ez
ils	**pay**ent

IMPERFECT
je	**pay**ais
tu	**pay**ais
il	**pay**ait
nous	**pay**ions
vous	**pay**iez
ils	**pay**aient

FUTURE
je	**pay**erai
tu	**pay**eras
il	**pay**era
nous	**pay**erons
vous	**pay**erez
ils	**pay**eront

IMPERATIVE
paye
payons
payez

CONDITIONAL
je	**pay**erais
tu	**pay**erais
il	**pay**erait
nous	**pay**erions
vous	**pay**eriez
ils	**pay**eraient

effrayer
to frighten

payer **70**
to pay

essayer
to try

PAST HISTORIC		*PRESENT SUBJUNCTIVE*	
je	**pay**ai	je	**pay**e
tu	**pay**as	tu	**pay**es
il	**pay**a	il	**pay**e
nous	**pay**âmes	nous	**pay**ions
vous	**pay**âtes	vous	**pay**iez
ils	**pay**èrent	ils	**pay**ent

PERFECT		*PAST SUBJUNCTIVE*	
j'	**ai pay**é	je	**pay**asse
tu	**as pay**é	tu	**pay**asses
il	**a pay**é	il	**pay**ât
nous	**avons pay**é	nous	**pay**assions
vous	**avez pay**é	vous	**pay**assiez
ils	**ont pay**é	ils	**pay**assent

CONSTRUCTIONS
être payé par chèque/à l'heure   to be paid by cheque/by the hour
est-ce qu'il t'a payé les billets?   did he pay you for the tickets?
il l'a payé 10 F   he paid 10 F for it
il l'a payé de sa vie   it cost him his life

71 peindre
to paint

PRESENT PARTICIPLE
peignant

PAST PARTICIPLE
peint

also **atteindre**
to reach

déteindre
to lose its colour

enfreindre
to infringe

PRESENT
- je **peins**
- tu **peins**
- il **peint**
- nous **peignons**
- vous **peignez**
- ils **peignent**

IMPERFECT
- je **peignais**
- tu **peignais**
- il **peignait**
- nous **peignions**
- vous **peigniez**
- ils **peignaient**

FUTURE
- je **peindrai**
- tu **peindras**
- il **peindra**
- nous **peindrons**
- vous **peindrez**
- ils **peindront**

IMPERATIVE
- **peins**
- **peignons**
- **peignez**

CONDITIONAL
- je **peindrais**
- tu **peindrais**
- il **peindrait**
- nous **peindrions**
- vous **peindriez**
- ils **peindraient**

to paint

éteindre
   to put out

teindre
   to dye

PAST HISTORIC
je	peignis
tu	peignis
il	peignit
nous	peignîmes
vous	peignîtes
ils	peignirent

PERFECT
j'	ai peint
tu	as peint
il	a peint
nous	avons peint
vous	avez peint
ils	ont peint

PRESENT SUBJUNCTIVE
je	peigne
tu	peignes
il	peigne
nous	peignions
vous	peigniez
ils	peignent

PAST SUBJUNCTIVE
je	peignisse
tu	peignisses
il	peignît
nous	peignissions
vous	peignissiez
ils	peignissent

CONSTRUCTIONS
peindre qch en bleu/à l'huile   to paint sth blue/in oils

72 perdre
to lose

PRESENT PARTICIPLE
perdant

PAST PARTICIPLE
perdu

PRESENT		*IMPERFECT*	
je	**perds**	je	**perdais**
tu	**perds**	tu	**perdais**
il	**perd**	il	**perdait**
nous	**perdons**	nous	**perdions**
vous	**perdez**	vous	**perdiez**
ils	**perdent**	ils	**perdaient**

		FUTURE	
		je	**perdrai**
		tu	**perdras**
		il	**perdra**
		nous	**perdrons**
		vous	**perdrez**
		ils	**perdront**

IMPERATIVE		*CONDITIONAL*	
	perds	je	**perdrais**
	perdons	tu	**perdrais**
	perdez	il	**perdrait**
		nous	**perdrions**
		vous	**perdriez**
		ils	**perdraient**

PAST HISTORIC
je	**perdis**
tu	**perdis**
il	**perdit**
nous	**perdîmes**
vous	**perdîtes**
ils	**perdirent**

PERFECT
j'	**ai perdu**
tu	**as perdu**
il	**a perdu**
nous	**avons perdu**
vous	**avez perdu**
ils	**ont perdu**

PRESENT SUBJUNCTIVE
je	**perde**
tu	**perdes**
il	**perde**
nous	**perdions**
vous	**perdiez**
ils	**perdent**

PAST SUBJUNCTIVE
je	**perdisse**
tu	**perdisses**
il	**perdît**
nous	**perdissions**
vous	**perdissiez**
ils	**perdissent**

CONSTRUCTIONS

perdre qn/qch de vue   to lose sight of sb/sth
perdre espoir/connaissance/du poids   to lose hope/consciousness/weight
tu perds ton temps à essayer   you're wasting your time trying
se perdre   to get lost; to disappear

73 permettre
to allow

PRESENT PARTICIPLE
permettant

PAST PARTICIPLE
permis

PRESENT		IMPERFECT	
je	**permets**	je	**permettais**
tu	**permets**	tu	**permettais**
il	**permet**	il	**permettait**
nous	**permettons**	nous	**permettions**
vous	**permettez**	vous	**permettiez**
ils	**permettent**	ils	**permettaient**

		FUTURE	
		je	**permettrai**
		tu	**permettras**
		il	**permettra**
		nous	**permettrons**
		vous	**permettrez**
		ils	**permettront**

IMPERATIVE		CONDITIONAL	
	permets	je	**permettrais**
	permettons	tu	**permettrais**
	permettez	il	**permettrait**
		nous	**permettrions**
		vous	**permettriez**
		ils	**permettraient**

PAST HISTORIC		PRESENT SUBJUNCTIVE	
je	permis	je	**permette**
tu	permis	tu	**permettes**
il	permit	il	**permette**
nous	permîmes	nous	**permettions**
vous	permîtes	vous	**permettiez**
ils	permirent	ils	**permettent**

PERFECT		PAST SUBJUNCTIVE	
j'	**ai** permis	je	permisse
tu	**as** permis	tu	permisses
il	**a** permis	il	permît
nous	**avons** permis	nous	permissions
vous	**avez** permis	vous	permissiez
ils	**ont** permis	ils	permissent

CONSTRUCTIONS

permettre à qn de faire qch   to allow sb to do sth
permettre qch à qn   to allow sb sth
mes moyens ne me le permettent pas   I can't afford it
permettez-moi de vous présenter ma sœur   may I
introduce my sister?

74 plaire

to please   *also* **déplaire**
to displease

PRESENT PARTICIPLE
plaisant

PAST PARTICIPLE
plu

PRESENT		*IMPERFECT*	
je	**plais**	je	**plaisais**
tu	**plais**	tu	**plaisais**
il	**plaît**	il	**plaisait**
nous	**plaisons**	nous	**plaisions**
vous	**plaisez**	vous	**plaisiez**
ils	**plaisent**	ils	**plaisaient**
		FUTURE	
		je	**plairai**
		tu	**plairas**
		il	**plaira**
		nous	**plairons**
		vous	**plairez**
		ils	**plairont**
IMPERATIVE		*CONDITIONAL*	
	plais	je	**plairais**
	plaisons	tu	**plairais**
	plaisez	il	**plairait**
		nous	**plairions**
		vous	**plairiez**
		ils	**plairaient**

to please

PAST HISTORIC			*PRESENT SUBJUNCTIVE*	
je	**plus**		je	**plaise**
tu	**plus**		tu	**plaises**
il	**plut**		il	**plaise**
nous	**plûmes**		nous	**plaisions**
vous	**plûtes**		vous	**plaisiez**
ils	**plurent**		ils	**plaisent**
PERFECT			*PAST SUBJUNCTIVE*	
j'	**ai** plu		je	**plusse**
tu	**as** plu		tu	**plusses**
il	**a** plu		il	**plût**
nous	**avons** plu		nous	**plussions**
vous	**avez** plu		vous	**plussiez**
ils	**ont** plu		ils	**plussent**

CONSTRUCTIONS
sa maison lui plaît   she likes her house
il cherche à plaire à tout le monde   he tries to please everybody
j'irai si ça me plaît   I'll go if I feel like it
s'il te plaît, s'il vous plaît   please
il se plaît à Paris   he likes being in Paris

75 pleuvoir
to rain

PRESENT PARTICIPLE
pleuvant

PAST PARTICIPLE
plu

PRESENT **il pleut**	*IMPERFECT* **il pleuvait**
	FUTURE **il pleuvra**
IMPERATIVE *not used*	*CONDITIONAL* **il pleuvrait**

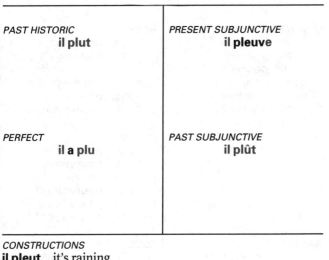

PAST HISTORIC **il plut**	*PRESENT SUBJUNCTIVE* **il pleuve**
PERFECT **il a plu**	*PAST SUBJUNCTIVE* **il plût**

CONSTRUCTIONS
il pleut   it's raining
il pleut à verse   it's pouring

76 pourvoir
to provide

PRESENT PARTICIPLE
pourvoyant

PAST PARTICIPLE
pourvu

PRESENT

je	**pourvois**
tu	**pourvois**
il	**pourvoit**
nous	**pourvoyons**
vous	**pourvoyez**
ils	**pourvoient**

IMPERFECT

je	**pourvoyais**
tu	**pourvoyais**
il	**pourvoyait**
nous	**pourvoyions**
vous	**pourvoyiez**
ils	**pourvoyaient**

FUTURE

je	**pourvoirai**
tu	**pourvoiras**
il	**pourvoira**
nous	**pourvoirons**
vous	**pourvoirez**
ils	**pourvoiront**

IMPERATIVE

pourvois
pourvoyons
pourvoyez

CONDITIONAL

je	**pourvoirais**
tu	**pourvoirais**
il	**pourvoirait**
nous	**pourvoirions**
vous	**pourvoiriez**
ils	**pourvoiraient**

PAST HISTORIC		PRESENT SUBJUNCTIVE	
je	**pourvus**	je	**pourvoie**
tu	**pourvus**	tu	**pourvoies**
il	**pourvut**	il	**pourvoie**
nous	**pourvûmes**	nous	**pourvoyions**
vous	**pourvûtes**	vous	**pourvoyiez**
ils	**pourvurent**	ils	**pourvoient**

PERFECT		PAST SUBJUNCTIVE	
j'	**ai pourvu**	je	**pourvusse**
tu	**as pourvu**	tu	**pourvusses**
il	**a pourvu**	il	**pourvût**
nous	**avons pourvu**	nous	**pourvussions**
vous	**avez pourvu**	vous	**pourvussiez**
ils	**ont pourvu**	ils	**pourvussent**

CONSTRUCTIONS

pourvoir qch de qch   to equip sth with sth
pourvoir aux besoins de qn   to provide for sb's needs

77 pouvoir
to be able

PRESENT PARTICIPLE
pouvant

PAST PARTICIPLE
pu

PRESENT

je	**peux**
tu	**peux**
il	**peut**
nous	**pouvons**
vous	**pouvez**
ils	**peuvent**

IMPERFECT

je	**pouvais**
tu	**pouvais**
il	**pouvait**
nous	**pouvions**
vous	**pouviez**
ils	**pouvaient**

FUTURE

je	**pourrai**
tu	**pourras**
il	**pourra**
nous	**pourrons**
vous	**pourrez**
ils	**pourront**

IMPERATIVE

not used

CONDITIONAL

je	**pourrais**
tu	**pourrais**
il	**pourrait**
nous	**pourrions**
vous	**pourriez**
ils	**pourraient**

to be able

PAST HISTORIC		PRESENT SUBJUNCTIVE	
je	pus	je	puisse
tu	pus	tu	puisses
il	put	il	puisse
nous	pûmes	nous	puissions
vous	pûtes	vous	puissiez
ils	purent	ils	puissent

PERFECT		PAST SUBJUNCTIVE	
j'	ai pu	je	pusse
tu	as pu	tu	pusses
il	a pu	il	pût
nous	avons pu	nous	pussions
vous	avez pu	vous	pussiez
ils	ont pu	ils	pussent

CONSTRUCTIONS

pouvoir faire to be able to do
il ne peut pas venir he can't come
il n'en peut plus he's tired out; he's had enough
il a été on ne peut plus aimable he couldn't have been kinder

78 prendre
to take

also **entreprendre**
to undertake

PRESENT PARTICIPLE
prenant

se méprendre
to be mistaken

PAST PARTICIPLE
pris

surprendre
to surprise

PRESENT		*IMPERFECT*	
je	**prends**	je	prenais
tu	**prends**	tu	prenais
il	**prend**	il	prenait
nous	prenons	nous	prenions
vous	prenez	vous	preniez
ils	prennent	ils	prenaient

FUTURE	
je	**prendrai**
tu	**prendras**
il	**prendra**
nous	**prendrons**
vous	**prendrez**
ils	**prendront**

IMPERATIVE	*CONDITIONAL*	
prends	je	**prendrais**
prenons	tu	**prendrais**
prenez	il	**prendrait**
	nous	**prendrions**
	vous	**prendriez**
	ils	**prendraient**

to take

PAST HISTORIC		PRESENT SUBJUNCTIVE	
je	pris	je	prenne
tu	pris	tu	prennes
il	prit	il	prenne
nous	prîmes	nous	prenions
vous	prîtes	vous	preniez
ils	prirent	ils	prennent

PERFECT		PAST SUBJUNCTIVE	
j'	ai pris	je	prisse
tu	as pris	tu	prisses
il	a pris	il	prît
nous	avons pris	nous	prissions
vous	avez pris	vous	prissiez
ils	ont pris	ils	prissent

CONSTRUCTIONS

prendre qch à qn   to take sth from sb
il l'a pris dans un tiroir/sur la table   he took it out of a drawer/from the table
prendre feu   to catch fire
prendre qn en amitié/en aversion   to take a liking/a dislike to sb

79 promettre

to promise   *also* **compromettre**
                             to compromise

PRESENT PARTICIPLE
promettant

PAST PARTICIPLE
promis

	PRESENT		*IMPERFECT*
je	**promets**	je	**promettais**
tu	**promets**	tu	**promettais**
il	**promet**	il	**promettait**
nous	**promettons**	nous	**promettions**
vous	**promettez**	vous	**promettiez**
ils	**promettent**	ils	**promettaient**

	FUTURE
je	**promettrai**
tu	**promettras**
il	**promettra**
nous	**promettrons**
vous	**promettrez**
ils	**promettront**

IMPERATIVE		*CONDITIONAL*
promets	je	**promettrais**
promettons	tu	**promettrais**
promettez	il	**promettrait**
	nous	**promettrions**
	vous	**promettriez**
	ils	**promettraient**

to promise

PAST HISTORIC		PRESENT SUBJUNCTIVE	
je	promis	je	promette
tu	promis	tu	promettes
il	promit	il	promette
nous	promîmes	nous	promettions
vous	promîtes	vous	promettiez
ils	promirent	ils	promettent

PERFECT		PAST SUBJUNCTIVE	
j'	ai promis	je	promisse
tu	as promis	tu	promisses
il	a promis	il	promît
nous	avons promis	nous	promissions
vous	avez promis	vous	promissiez
ils	ont promis	ils	promissent

CONSTRUCTIONS

promettre qch à qn   to promise sth to sb
promettre à qn de faire qch   to promise sb that one will do sth
on nous promet du beau temps   we're in for some fine weather, they say
se promettre de faire   to resolve to do

80 protéger
to protect

also **abréger**
to shorten

PRESENT PARTICIPLE
protégeant

alléger
to lighten

PAST PARTICIPLE
protégé

assiéger
to besiege

PRESENT
je	protège
tu	protèges
il	protège
nous	protégeons
vous	protégez
ils	protègent

IMPERFECT
je	protégeais
tu	protégeais
il	protégeait
nous	protégions
vous	protégiez
ils	protégeaient

FUTURE
je	protégerai
tu	protégeras
il	protégera
nous	protégerons
vous	protégerez
ils	protégeront

IMPERATIVE
protège
protégeons
protégez

CONDITIONAL
je	protégerais
tu	protégerais
il	protégerait
nous	protégerions
vous	protégeriez
ils	protégeraient

piéger
to booby-trap

PAST HISTORIC		PRESENT SUBJUNCTIVE	
je	**protég**eai	je	**protèg**e
tu	**protég**eas	tu	**protèg**es
il	**protég**ea	il	**protèg**e
nous	**protég**eâmes	nous	**protég**ions
vous	**protég**eâtes	vous	**protég**iez
ils	**protég**èrent	ils	**protèg**ent
PERFECT		**PAST SUBJUNCTIVE**	
j'	**ai protégé**	je	**protég**easse
tu	**as protégé**	tu	**protég**easses
il	**a protégé**	il	**protég**eât
nous	**avons protégé**	nous	**protég**eassions
vous	**avez protégé**	vous	**protég**eassiez
ils	**ont protégé**	ils	**protég**eassent

CONSTRUCTIONS
se protéger de qch/contre qch   to protect oneself from
sth/against sth

81 recevoir
to receive

also **apercevoir**
to see

PRESENT PARTICIPLE
recevant

décevoir
to disappoint

PAST PARTICIPLE
reçu

percevoir
to perceive

PRESENT
je	**reçois**
tu	**reçois**
il	**reçoit**
nous	**recevons**
vous	**recevez**
ils	**reçoivent**

IMPERFECT
je	**recevais**
tu	**recevais**
il	**recevait**
nous	**recevions**
vous	**receviez**
ils	**recevaient**

FUTURE
je	**recevrai**
tu	**recevras**
il	**recevra**
nous	**recevrons**
vous	**recevrez**
ils	**recevront**

IMPERATIVE
reçois
recevons
recevez

CONDITIONAL
je	**recevrais**
tu	**recevrais**
il	**recevrait**
nous	**recevrions**
vous	**recevriez**
ils	**recevraient**

PAST HISTORIC		PRESENT SUBJUNCTIVE	
je	reçus	je	reçoive
tu	reçus	tu	reçoives
il	reçut	il	reçoive
nous	reçûmes	nous	**recev**ions
vous	reçûtes	vous	**recev**iez
ils	reçurent	ils	reçoivent
PERFECT		PAST SUBJUNCTIVE	
j'	**ai** reçu	je	reçusse
tu	**as** reçu	tu	reçusses
il	**a** reçu	il	reçût
nous	**avons** reçu	nous	reçussions
vous	**avez** reçu	vous	reçussiez
ils	**ont** reçu	ils	reçussent

CONSTRUCTIONS

recevoir un cadeau de qn to receive a present from sb
être reçu à un examen to pass an exam
être reçu à l'université to get a place at university
il a reçu un coup de pied he got kicked

82 rendre
to give back

PRESENT PARTICIPLE
rendant

PAST PARTICIPLE
rendu

PRESENT		*IMPERFECT*	
je	**rends**	je	**rendais**
tu	**rends**	tu	**rendais**
il	**rend**	il	**rendait**
nous	**rendons**	nous	**rendions**
vous	**rendez**	vous	**rendiez**
ils	**rendent**	ils	**rendaient**

		FUTURE	
		je	**rendrai**
		tu	**rendras**
		il	**rendra**
		nous	**rendrons**
		vous	**rendrez**
		ils	**rendront**

IMPERATIVE		*CONDITIONAL*	
rends		je	**rendrais**
rendons		tu	**rendrais**
rendez		il	**rendrait**
		nous	**rendrions**
		vous	**rendriez**
		ils	**rendraient**

to give back

PAST HISTORIC		PRESENT SUBJUNCTIVE	
je	rendis	je	rende
tu	rendis	tu	rendes
il	rendit	il	rende
nous	rendîmes	nous	rendions
vous	rendîtes	vous	rendiez
ils	rendirent	ils	rendent

PERFECT		PAST SUBJUNCTIVE	
j'	ai rendu	je	rendisse
tu	as rendu	tu	rendisses
il	a rendu	il	rendît
nous	avons rendu	nous	rendissions
vous	avez rendu	vous	rendissiez
ils	ont rendu	ils	rendissent

CONSTRUCTIONS

rendre qch à qn to give sth back to sb
rendre qn heureux to make sb happy
rendre visite à qn to pay sb a visit
se rendre to surrender
se rendre compte de qch to realize sth

83 rentrer

to go back; to go in

PRESENT PARTICIPLE
rentrant

PAST PARTICIPLE
rentré

PRESENT

je	**rentre**
tu	**rentres**
il	**rentre**
nous	**rentrons**
vous	**rentrez**
ils	**rentrent**

IMPERFECT

je	**rentrais**
tu	**rentrais**
il	**rentrait**
nous	**rentrions**
vous	**rentriez**
ils	**rentraient**

FUTURE

je	**rentrerai**
tu	**rentreras**
il	**rentrera**
nous	**rentrerons**
vous	**rentrerez**
ils	**rentreront**

IMPERATIVE

rentre
rentrons
rentrez

CONDITIONAL

je	**rentrerais**
tu	**rentrerais**
il	**rentrerait**
nous	**rentrerions**
vous	**rentreriez**
ils	**rentreraient**

to go back; to go in

PAST HISTORIC		PRESENT SUBJUNCTIVE	
je	**rentrai**	je	**rentre**
tu	**rentras**	tu	**rentres**
il	**rentra**	il	**rentre**
nous	**rentrâmes**	nous	**rentrions**
vous	**rentrâtes**	vous	**rentriez**
ils	**rentrèrent**	ils	**rentrent**

PERFECT		PAST SUBJUNCTIVE	
je	**suis rentré**	je	**rentrasse**
tu	**es rentré**	tu	**rentrasses**
il	**est rentré**	il	**rentrât**
nous	**sommes rentrés**	nous	**rentrassions**
vous	**êtes rentré(s)**	vous	**rentrassiez**
ils	**sont rentrés**	ils	**rentrassent**

CONSTRUCTIONS
rentrer à la maison   to go back home
rentrer dans une firme   to join a firm
rentrer dans un arbre   to crash into a tree
il a rentré la voiture   he put the car away
rentrer ses griffes   to draw in one's claws

84 répondre
to answer

also **confondre**
to confuse

PRESENT PARTICIPLE
répondant

correspondre
to correspond

PAST PARTICIPLE
répondu

tondre
to shear

PRESENT		*IMPERFECT*

PRESENT
je	**réponds**
tu	**réponds**
il	**répond**
nous	**répondons**
vous	**répondez**
ils	**répondent**

IMPERFECT
je	**répondais**
tu	**répondais**
il	**répondait**
nous	**répondions**
vous	**répondiez**
ils	**répondaient**

FUTURE
je	**répondrai**
tu	**répondras**
il	**répondra**
nous	**répondrons**
vous	**répondrez**
ils	**répondront**

IMPERATIVE
réponds
répondons
répondez

CONDITIONAL
je	**répondrais**
tu	**répondrais**
il	**répondrait**
nous	**répondrions**
vous	**répondriez**
ils	**répondraient**

to answer

PAST HISTORIC		PRESENT SUBJUNCTIVE	
je	**répond**is	je	**répond**e
tu	**répond**is	tu	**répond**es
il	**répond**it	il	**répond**e
nous	**répond**îmes	nous	**répond**ions
vous	**répond**îtes	vous	**répond**iez
ils	**répond**irent	ils	**répond**ent

PERFECT		PAST SUBJUNCTIVE	
j'	ai **répond**u	je	**répond**isse
tu	as **répond**u	tu	**répond**isses
il	a **répond**u	il	**répond**ît
nous	avons **répond**u	nous	**répond**issions
vous	avez **répond**u	vous	**répond**issiez
ils	ont **répond**u	ils	**répond**issent

CONSTRUCTIONS

répondre à qn / à une question   to answer sb/a question
on a sonné – va répondre   that's the bell – go and answer the door
ça ne répond pas   there's no reply
répondre de qn   to answer for sb

85 résoudre
to solve

PRESENT PARTICIPLE
résolvant

PAST PARTICIPLE
résolu

PRESENT		*IMPERFECT*	
je	**résous**	je	**résolvais**
tu	**résous**	tu	**résolvais**
il	**résout**	il	**résolvait**
nous	**résolvons**	nous	**résolvions**
vous	**résolvez**	vous	**résolviez**
ils	**résolvent**	ils	**résolvaient**

		FUTURE	
		je	**résoudrai**
		tu	**résoudras**
		il	**résoudra**
		nous	**résoudrons**
		vous	**résoudrez**
		ils	**résoudront**

IMPERATIVE	*CONDITIONAL*	
résous	je	**résoudrais**
résolvons	tu	**résoudrais**
résolvez	il	**résoudrait**
	nous	**résoudrions**
	vous	**résoudriez**
	ils	**résoudraient**

to solve

PAST HISTORIC		PRESENT SUBJUNCTIVE	
je	résolus	je	résolve
tu	résolus	tu	résolves
il	résolut	il	résolve
nous	résolûmes	nous	résolvions
vous	résolûtes	vous	résolviez
ils	résolurent	ils	résolvent

PERFECT		PAST SUBJUNCTIVE	
j'	ai résolu	je	résolusse
tu	as résolu	tu	résolusses
il	a résolu	il	résolût
nous	avons résolu	nous	résolussions
vous	avez résolu	vous	résolussiez
ils	ont résolu	ils	résolussent

CONSTRUCTIONS

se résoudre à faire qch   to resolve to do sth
être résolu à faire   to be set on doing

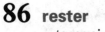

86 rester

to remain

PRESENT PARTICIPLE
restant

PAST PARTICIPLE
resté

PRESENT		*IMPERFECT*	
je	**reste**	je	**rest**ais
tu	**restes**	tu	**rest**ais
il	**reste**	il	**rest**ait
nous	**restons**	nous	**rest**ions
vous	**restez**	vous	**rest**iez
ils	**restent**	ils	**rest**aient

		FUTURE	
		je	**rester**ai
		tu	**rester**as
		il	**rester**a
		nous	**rester**ons
		vous	**rester**ez
		ils	**rester**ont

IMPERATIVE		*CONDITIONAL*	
	reste	je	**rester**ais
	restons	tu	**rester**ais
	restez	il	**rester**ait
		nous	**rester**ions
		vous	**rester**iez
		ils	**rester**aient

rester 86
to remain

PAST HISTORIC		*PRESENT SUBJUNCTIVE*	
je	**rest**ai	je	**rest**e
tu	**rest**as	tu	**rest**es
il	**rest**a	il	**rest**e
nous	**rest**âmes	nous	**rest**ions
vous	**rest**âtes	vous	**rest**iez
ils	**rest**èrent	ils	**rest**ent

PERFECT		*PAST SUBJUNCTIVE*	
je	suis **rest**é	je	**rest**asse
tu	es **rest**é	tu	**rest**asses
il	est **rest**é	il	**rest**ât
nous	sommes **rest**és	nous	**rest**assions
vous	êtes **rest**é(s)	vous	**rest**assiez
ils	sont **rest**és	ils	**rest**assent

CONSTRUCTIONS

il est resté à regarder la télévision   he stayed watching
television
c'est tout l'argent qui leur reste   that's all the money they
have left
il reste encore un peu de pain   there's still a little bread
left

87 retourner
to return

PRESENT PARTICIPLE
retournant

PAST PARTICIPLE
retourné

PRESENT		*IMPERFECT*	
je	**retourne**	je	**retournais**
tu	**retournes**	tu	**retournais**
il	**retourne**	il	**retournait**
nous	**retournons**	nous	**retournions**
vous	**retournez**	vous	**retourniez**
ils	**retournent**	ils	**retournaient**

		FUTURE	
		je	**retournerai**
		tu	**retourneras**
		il	**retournera**
		nous	**retournerons**
		vous	**retournerez**
		ils	**retourneront**

IMPERATIVE		*CONDITIONAL*	
	retourne	je	**retournerais**
	retournons	tu	**retournerais**
	retournez	il	**retournerait**
		nous	**retournerions**
		vous	**retourneriez**
		ils	**retourneraient**

to return

PAST HISTORIC		PRESENT SUBJUNCTIVE	
je	**retournai**	je	**retourne**
tu	**retournas**	tu	**retournes**
il	**retourna**	il	**retourne**
nous	**retournâmes**	nous	**retournions**
vous	**retournâtes**	vous	**retourniez**
ils	**retournèrent**	ils	**retournent**

PERFECT		PAST SUBJUNCTIVE	
je	**suis retourné**	je	**retournasse**
tu	**es retourné**	tu	**retournasses**
il	**est retourné**	il	**retournât**
nous	**sommes retournés**	nous	**retournassions**
vous	**êtes retourné(s)**	vous	**retournassiez**
ils	**sont retournés**	ils	**retournassent**

CONSTRUCTIONS

il a retourné le seau/sac he turned the bucket upside down/the bag inside out
il a retourné les marchandises he sent the goods back
retourner en Italie to go back to Italy
se retourner to turn over; to turn round

88 revenir
to come back

PRESENT PARTICIPLE
revenant

PAST PARTICIPLE
revenu

PRESENT
je	**reviens**
tu	**reviens**
il	**revient**
nous	**reven**ons
vous	**reven**ez
ils	**reviennent**

IMPERFECT
je	**reven**ais
tu	**reven**ais
il	**reven**ait
nous	**reven**ions
vous	**reven**iez
ils	**reven**aient

FUTURE
je	**reviendrai**
tu	**reviendras**
il	**reviendra**
nous	**reviendrons**
vous	**reviendrez**
ils	**reviendront**

IMPERATIVE
reviens
revenons
revenez

CONDITIONAL
je	**reviendrais**
tu	**reviendrais**
il	**reviendrait**
nous	**reviendrions**
vous	**reviendriez**
ils	**reviendraient**

PAST HISTORIC		PRESENT SUBJUNCTIVE	
je	revins	je	revienne
tu	revins	tu	reviennes
il	revint	il	revienne
nous	revînmes	nous	revenions
vous	revîntes	vous	reveniez
ils	revinrent	ils	reviennent

PERFECT		PAST SUBJUNCTIVE	
je	suis revenu	je	revinsse
tu	es revenu	tu	revinsses
il	est revenu	il	revînt
nous	sommes revenus	nous	revinssions
vous	êtes revenu(s)	vous	revinssiez
ils	sont revenus	ils	revinssent

CONSTRUCTIONS

le repas revient à 70 F   the meal comes to 70 F
il est revenu à Paris   he came back to Paris
il est revenu de Paris   he's back from Paris
revenir sur une promesse   to go back on a promise
revenir sur ses pas   to retrace one's steps

89 rire

to laugh   *also* **sourire**
to smile

PRESENT PARTICIPLE
riant

PAST PARTICIPLE
ri

PRESENT
je **ris**
tu **ris**
il **rit**
nous **rions**
vous **riez**
ils **rient**

IMPERFECT
je **riais**
tu **riais**
il **riait**
nous **riions**
vous **riiez**
ils **riaient**

FUTURE
je **rirai**
tu **riras**
il **rira**
nous **rirons**
vous **rirez**
ils **riront**

IMPERATIVE
ris
rions
riez

CONDITIONAL
je **rirais**
tu **rirais**
il **rirait**
nous **ririons**
vous **ririez**
ils **riraient**

PAST HISTORIC		*PRESENT SUBJUNCTIVE*	
je	**ris**	je	**rie**
tu	**ris**	tu	**ries**
il	**rit**	il	**rie**
nous	**rîmes**	nous	**riions**
vous	**rîtes**	vous	**riiez**
ils	**rirent**	ils	**rient**

PERFECT		*PAST SUBJUNCTIVE*	
j'	**ai** ri	je	**risse**
tu	**as** ri	tu	**risses**
il	**a** ri	il	**rît**
nous	**avons** ri	nous	**rissions**
vous	**avez** ri	vous	**rissiez**
ils	**ont** ri	ils	**rissent**

CONSTRUCTIONS

rire de qn / qch   to laugh at sb/sth
il a fait cela pour rire   he did it for a joke
rire aux éclats   to roar with laughter

90 rompre
to break

also **corrompre**
to corrupt

PRESENT PARTICIPLE
rompant

interrompre
to interrupt

PAST PARTICIPLE
rompu

PRESENT

je	**romps**
tu	**romps**
il	**rompt**
nous	**rompons**
vous	**rompez**
ils	**rompent**

IMPERFECT

je	**rompais**
tu	**rompais**
il	**rompait**
nous	**rompions**
vous	**rompiez**
ils	**rompaient**

FUTURE

je	**romprai**
tu	**rompras**
il	**rompra**
nous	**romprons**
vous	**romprez**
ils	**rompront**

IMPERATIVE

romps
rompons
rompez

CONDITIONAL

je	**romprais**
tu	**romprais**
il	**romprait**
nous	**romprions**
vous	**rompriez**
ils	**rompraient**

PAST HISTORIC		*PRESENT SUBJUNCTIVE*	
je	rompis	je	rompe
tu	rompis	tu	rompes
il	rompit	il	rompe
nous	rompîmes	nous	rompions
vous	rompîtes	vous	rompiez
ils	rompirent	ils	rompent

PERFECT		*PAST SUBJUNCTIVE*	
j'	ai rompu	je	rompisse
tu	as rompu	tu	rompisses
il	a rompu	il	rompît
nous	avons rompu	nous	rompissions
vous	avez rompu	vous	rompissiez
ils	ont rompu	ils	rompissent

CONSTRUCTIONS

ils ont rompu (leurs fiançailles)   they've broken off their engagement

rompre les rangs   to fall out

se rompre   to break; to burst

être rompu (de fatigue)   to be exhausted

91 savoir
to know

PRESENT PARTICIPLE
sachant

PAST PARTICIPLE
su

PRESENT
je	**sais**
tu	**sais**
il	**sait**
nous	**savons**
vous	**savez**
ils	**savent**

IMPERFECT
je	**savais**
tu	**savais**
il	**savait**
nous	**savions**
vous	**saviez**
ils	**savaient**

FUTURE
je	**saurai**
tu	**sauras**
il	**saura**
nous	**saurons**
vous	**saurez**
ils	**sauront**

IMPERATIVE
sache
sachons
sachez

CONDITIONAL
je	**saurais**
tu	**saurais**
il	**saurait**
nous	**saurions**
vous	**sauriez**
ils	**sauraient**

PAST HISTORIC		PRESENT SUBJUNCTIVE	
je	sus	je	sache
tu	sus	tu	saches
il	sut	il	sache
nous	sûmes	nous	sachions
vous	sûtes	vous	sachiez
ils	surent	ils	sachent

PERFECT		PAST SUBJUNCTIVE	
j'	ai su	je	susse
tu	as su	tu	susses
il	a su	il	sût
nous	avons su	nous	sussions
vous	avez su	vous	sussiez
ils	ont su	ils	sussent

CONSTRUCTIONS

savoir faire   to know how to do; to be able to do
je ne sais pas quoi faire   I don't know what to do
je vous ferai savoir   I'll let you know
à savoir   that is, namely
on ne sait jamais   you never can tell

92 sentir

to smell; to feel *also* **consentir**
to agree

PRESENT PARTICIPLE
sentant

démentir
to deny

PAST PARTICIPLE
senti

mentir
to lie

PRESENT		IMPERFECT	
je	**sens**	je	**sentais**
tu	**sens**	tu	**sentais**
il	**sent**	il	**sentait**
nous	**sentons**	nous	**sentions**
vous	**sentez**	vous	**sentiez**
ils	**sentent**	ils	**sentaient**

		FUTURE	
		je	**sentirai**
		tu	**sentiras**
		il	**sentira**
		nous	**sentirons**
		vous	**sentirez**
		ils	**sentiront**

IMPERATIVE		CONDITIONAL	
	sens	je	**sentirais**
	sentons	tu	**sentirais**
	sentez	il	**sentirait**
		nous	**sentirions**
		vous	**sentiriez**
		ils	**sentiraient**

to smell; to feel

ressentir
to feel

PAST HISTORIC		PRESENT SUBJUNCTIVE	
je	sentis	je	sente
tu	sentis	tu	sentes
il	sentit	il	sente
nous	sentîmes	nous	sentions
vous	sentîtes	vous	sentiez
ils	sentirent	ils	sentent

PERFECT		PAST SUBJUNCTIVE	
j'	ai senti	je	sentisse
tu	as senti	tu	sentisses
il	a senti	il	sentît
nous	avons senti	nous	sentissions
vous	avez senti	vous	sentissiez
ils	ont senti	ils	sentissent

CONSTRUCTIONS

sentir bon/mauvais   to smell good *or* nice/bad
j'ai senti s'arrêter la voiture   I felt the car stopping
se sentir mal/mieux   to feel ill/better

93 servir
to serve

PRESENT PARTICIPLE
servant

PAST PARTICIPLE
servi

PRESENT		*IMPERFECT*
je **sers**		je **servais**
tu **sers**		tu **servais**
il **sert**		il **servait**
nous **servons**		nous **servions**
vous **servez**		vous **serviez**
ils **servent**		ils **servaient**

FUTURE
je **servirai**
tu **serviras**
il **servira**
nous **servirons**
vous **servirez**
ils **serviront**

IMPERATIVE
sers
servons
servez

CONDITIONAL
je **servirais**
tu **servirais**
il **servirait**
nous **servirions**
vous **serviriez**
ils **serviraient**

PAST HISTORIC		PRESENT SUBJUNCTIVE	
je	**servis**	je	**serve**
tu	**servis**	tu	**serves**
il	**servit**	il	**serve**
nous	**servîmes**	nous	**servions**
vous	**servîtes**	vous	**serviez**
ils	**servirent**	ils	**servent**

PERFECT		PAST SUBJUNCTIVE	
j'	**ai servi**	je	**servisse**
tu	**as servi**	tu	**servisses**
il	**a servi**	il	**servît**
nous	**avons servi**	nous	**servissions**
vous	**avez servi**	vous	**servissiez**
ils	**ont servi**	ils	**servissent**

CONSTRUCTIONS

servir un plat à qn   to serve sb with a dish
servir à qn/à qch   to be useful to sb/for sth
servir à faire   to be used for doing
à quoi sert de pleurer?   what's the use of crying?
servir de   to act as; to serve as
se servir d'un plat   to help oneself to a dish

94 songer
to think

also **plonger**
to dive

prolonger
to prolong

rallonger
to lengthen

PRESENT PARTICIPLE
songeant

PAST PARTICIPLE
songé

PRESENT

je	**songe**
tu	**songes**
il	**songe**
nous	**songeons**
vous	**songez**
ils	**songent**

IMPERFECT

je	**songeais**
tu	**songeais**
il	**songeait**
nous	**songions**
vous	**songiez**
ils	**songeaient**

FUTURE

je	**songerai**
tu	**songeras**
il	**songera**
nous	**songerons**
vous	**songerez**
ils	**songeront**

IMPERATIVE

songe
songeons
songez

CONDITIONAL

je	**songerais**
tu	**songerais**
il	**songerait**
nous	**songerions**
vous	**songeriez**
ils	**songeraient**

ronger
to gnaw

PAST HISTORIC		PRESENT SUBJUNCTIVE	
je	**song**eai	je	**song**e
tu	**song**eas	tu	**song**es
il	**song**ea	il	**song**e
nous	**song**eâmes	nous	**song**ions
vous	**song**eâtes	vous	**song**iez
ils	**song**èrent	ils	**song**ent

PERFECT		PAST SUBJUNCTIVE	
j'	**ai songé**	je	**song**easse
tu	**as songé**	tu	**song**easses
il	**a songé**	il	**song**eât
nous	**avons songé**	nous	**song**eassions
vous	**avez songé**	vous	**song**eassiez
ils	**ont songé**	ils	**song**eassent

CONSTRUCTIONS
songer à qch   to think sth over; to think of sth
songer à faire qch   to contemplate doing sth

95 sortir

to go out   *also* **ressortir**

to stand out

PRESENT PARTICIPLE
sortant

PAST PARTICIPLE
sorti

PRESENT

je	sors
tu	sors
il	sort
nous	sortons
vous	sortez
ils	sortent

IMPERFECT

je	sortais
tu	sortais
il	sortait
nous	sortions
vous	sortiez
ils	sortaient

FUTURE

je	sortirai
tu	sortiras
il	sortira
nous	sortirons
vous	sortirez
ils	sortiront

IMPERATIVE

sors
sortons
sortez

CONDITIONAL

je	sortirais
tu	sortirais
il	sortirait
nous	sortirions
vous	sortiriez
ils	sortiraient

PAST HISTORIC		*PRESENT SUBJUNCTIVE*	
je	**sortis**	je	**sorte**
tu	**sortis**	tu	**sortes**
il	**sortit**	il	**sorte**
nous	**sortîmes**	nous	**sortions**
vous	**sortîtes**	vous	**sortiez**
ils	**sortirent**	ils	**sortent**
PERFECT		*PAST SUBJUNCTIVE*	
je	**suis sorti**	je	**sortisse**
tu	**es sorti**	tu	**sortisses**
il	**est sorti**	il	**sortît**
nous	**sommes sortis**	nous	**sortissions**
vous	**êtes sorti(s)**	vous	**sortissiez**
ils	**sont sortis**	ils	**sortissent**

CONSTRUCTIONS

sortir d'une pièce/d'un pays to go (*or* come) out of a room/leave a country
il a sorti la voiture du garage he got the car out of the garage
sortir le chien to take the dog out

96 se souvenir
to remember

PRESENT PARTICIPLE
se souvenant

PAST PARTICIPLE
souvenu

PRESENT

je	**me souviens**
tu	**te souviens**
il	**se souvient**
nous	**nous souvenons**
vous	**vous souvenez**
ils	**se souviennent**

IMPERFECT

je	**me souvenais**
tu	**te souvenais**
il	**se souvenait**
nous	**nous souvenions**
vous	**vous souveniez**
ils	**se souvenaient**

FUTURE

je	**me souviendrai**
tu	**te souviendras**
il	**se souviendra**
nous	**nous souviendrons**
vous	**vous souviendrez**
ils	**se souviendront**

IMPERATIVE

souviens-toi
souvenons-nous
souvenez-vous

CONDITIONAL

je	**me souviendrais**
tu	**te souviendrais**
il	**se souviendrait**
nous	**nous souviendrions**
vous	**vous souviendriez**
ils	**se souviendraient**

PAST HISTORIC		*PRESENT SUBJUNCTIVE*	
je	**me souvins**	je	**me souvienne**
tu	**te souvins**	tu	**te souviennes**
il	**se souvint**	il	**se souvienne**
nous	**nous souvînmes**	nous	**nous souvenions**
vous	**vous souvîntes**	vous	**vous souveniez**
ils	**se souvinrent**	ils	**se souviennent**

PERFECT		*PAST SUBJUNCTIVE*	
je	**me suis souvenu**	je	**me souvinsse**
tu	**t'es souvenu**	tu	**te souvinsses**
il	**s'est souvenu**	il	**se souvînt**
nous	**nous sommes souvenus**	nous	**nous souvinssions**
vous	**vous êtes souvenu(s)**	vous	**vous souvinssiez**
ils	**se sont souvenus**	ils	**se souvinssent**

CONSTRUCTIONS
se souvenir de qn/qch   to remember sb/sth
se souvenir d'avoir fait qch   to remember doing sth

97 suffire
to be enough

PRESENT PARTICIPLE
suffisant

PAST PARTICIPLE
suffi

PRESENT		IMPERFECT	
je	**suffis**	je	**suffisais**
tu	**suffis**	tu	**suffisais**
il	**suffit**	il	**suffisait**
nous	**suffisons**	nous	**suffisions**
vous	**suffisez**	vous	**suffisiez**
ils	**suffisent**	ils	**suffisaient**

		FUTURE	
		je	**suffirai**
		tu	**suffiras**
		il	**suffira**
		nous	**suffirons**
		vous	**suffirez**
		ils	**suffiront**

IMPERATIVE	CONDITIONAL	
suffis	je	**suffirais**
suffisons	tu	**suffirais**
suffisez	il	**suffirait**
	nous	**suffirions**
	vous	**suffiriez**
	ils	**suffiraient**

PAST HISTORIC		*PRESENT SUBJUNCTIVE*	
je	**suffis**	je	**suffise**
tu	**suffis**	tu	**suffises**
il	**suffit**	il	**suffise**
nous	**suffîmes**	nous	**suffisions**
vous	**suffîtes**	vous	**suffisiez**
ils	**suffirent**	ils	**suffisent**
PERFECT		*PAST SUBJUNCTIVE*	
j'	**ai suffi**	je	**suffisse**
tu	**as suffi**	tu	**suffisses**
il	**a suffi**	il	**suffît**
nous	**avons suffi**	nous	**suffissions**
vous	**avez suffi**	vous	**suffissiez**
ils	**ont suffi**	ils	**suffissent**

CONSTRUCTIONS
suffire à *or* **pour faire**   to be sufficient *or* enough to do
suffire à qn   to be enough for sb
(ça) suffit!   that's enough!, that will do!
il suffit de 2 heures pour y aller   2 hours is enough to get there

98 .suivre
to follow   *also* **poursuivre**
                    to pursue

PRESENT PARTICIPLE
suivant

PAST PARTICIPLE
suivi

PRESENT
je **suis**
tu **suis**
il **suit**
nous **suivons**
vous **suivez**
ils **suivent**

IMPERFECT
je **suivais**
tu **suivais**
il **suivait**
nous **suivions**
vous **suiviez**
ils **suivaient**

FUTURE
je **suivrai**
tu **suivras**
il **suivra**
nous **suivrons**
vous **suivrez**
ils **suivront**

IMPERATIVE
suis
suivons
suivez

CONDITIONAL
je **suivrais**
tu **suivrais**
il **suivrait**
nous **suivrions**
vous **suivriez**
ils **suivraient**

PAST HISTORIC		PRESENT SUBJUNCTIVE	
je	suivis	je	suive
tu	suivis	tu	suives
il	suivit	il	suive
nous	suivîmes	nous	suivions
vous	suivîtes	vous	suiviez
ils	suivirent	ils	suivent

PERFECT		PAST SUBJUNCTIVE	
j'	ai suivi	je	suivisse
tu	as suivi	tu	suivisses
il	a suivi	il	suivît
nous	avons suivi	nous	suivissions
vous	avez suivi	vous	suivissiez
ils	ont suivi	ils	suivissent

CONSTRUCTIONS

suivre un régime   to be on a diet
suivre une classe   to attend a class
faire suivre son courrier   to have one's mail forwarded

99 surseoir
to defer

PRESENT PARTICIPLE
sursoyant

PAST PARTICIPLE
sursis

	PRESENT		IMPERFECT
je	**sursois**	je	**sursoyais**
tu	**sursois**	tu	**sursoyais**
il	**sursoit**	il	**sursoyait**
nous	**sursoyons**	nous	**sursoyions**
vous	**sursoyez**	vous	**sursoyiez**
ils	**sursoient**	ils	**sursoyaient**

			FUTURE
		je	**surseoirai**
		tu	**surseoiras**
		il	**surseoira**
		nous	**surseoirons**
		vous	**surseoirez**
		ils	**surseoiront**

IMPERATIVE		CONDITIONAL
sursois	je	**surseoirais**
sursoyons	tu	**surseoirais**
sursoyez	il	**surseoirait**
	nous	**surseoirions**
	vous	**surseoiriez**
	ils	**surseoiraient**

to defer

PAST HISTORIC		PRESENT SUBJUNCTIVE	
je	**sursis**	je	**sursoie**
tu	**sursis**	tu	**sursoies**
il	**sursit**	il	**sursoie**
nous	**sursîmes**	nous	**sursoyions**
vous	**sursîtes**	vous	**sursoyiez**
ils	**sursirent**	ils	**sursoient**

PERFECT		PAST SUBJUNCTIVE	
j'	**ai sursis**	je	**sursisse**
tu	**as sursis**	tu	**sursisses**
il	**a sursis**	il	**sursît**
nous	**avons sursis**	nous	**sursissions**
vous	**avez sursis**	vous	**sursissiez**
ils	**ont sursis**	ils	**sursissent**

CONSTRUCTIONS

surseoir à qch   to defer *or* postpone sth

100 se taire
to stop talking

PRESENT PARTICIPLE
se taisant

PAST PARTICIPLE
tu

PRESENT			*IMPERFECT*	
je	**me tais**		je	**me taisais**
tu	**te tais**		tu	**te taisais**
il	**se tait**		il	**se taisait**
nous	**nous taisons**		nous	**nous taisions**
vous	**vous taisez**		vous	**vous taisiez**
ils	**se taisent**		ils	**se taisaient**

			FUTURE	
			je	**me tairai**
			tu	**te tairas**
			il	**se taira**
			nous	**nous tairons**
			vous	**vous tairez**
			ils	**se tairont**

IMPERATIVE		*CONDITIONAL*	
tais-toi		je	**me tairais**
taisons-nous		tu	**te tairais**
taisez-vous		il	**se tairait**
		nous	**nous tairions**
		vous	**vous tairiez**
		ils	**se tairaient**

to stop talking

PAST HISTORIC		PRESENT SUBJUNCTIVE	
je	**me tus**	je	**me taise**
tu	**te tus**	tu	**te taises**
il	**se tut**	il	**se taise**
nous	**nous tûmes**	nous	**nous taisions**
vous	**vous tûtes**	vous	**vous taisiez**
ils	**se turent**	ils	**se taisent**

PERFECT		PAST SUBJUNCTIVE	
je	**me suis** tu	je	**me tusse**
tu	**t'es** tu	tu	**te tusses**
il	**s'est** tu	il	**se tût**
nous	**nous sommes** tus	nous	**nous tussions**
vous	**vous êtes** tu(s)	vous	**vous tussiez**
ils	**se sont** tus	ils	**se tussent**

CONSTRUCTIONS
ils se sont tus they stopped talking
taisez-vous! be quiet!
se taire sur qch to keep quiet about sth

101 tenir

to hold

also **appartenir**
to belong

contenir
to contain

entretenir
to maintain

PRESENT PARTICIPLE
tenant

PAST PARTICIPLE
tenu

PRESENT	
je	**tiens**
tu	**tiens**
il	**tient**
nous	**tenons**
vous	**tenez**
ils	**tiennent**

IMPERFECT	
je	**tenais**
tu	**tenais**
il	**tenait**
nous	**tenions**
vous	**teniez**
ils	**tenaient**

FUTURE	
je	**tiendrai**
tu	**tiendras**
il	**tiendra**
nous	**tiendrons**
vous	**tiendrez**
ils	**tiendront**

IMPERATIVE
tiens
tenons
tenez

CONDITIONAL	
je	**tiendrais**
tu	**tiendrais**
il	**tiendrait**
nous	**tiendrions**
vous	**tiendriez**
ils	**tiendraient**

soutenir
to support

PAST HISTORIC		PRESENT SUBJUNCTIVE	
je	tins	je	tienne
tu	tins	tu	tiennes
il	tint	il	tienne
nous	tînmes	nous	tenions
vous	tîntes	vous	teniez
ils	tinrent	ils	tiennent

PERFECT		PAST SUBJUNCTIVE	
j'	ai tenu	je	tinsse
tu	as tenu	tu	tinsses
il	a tenu	il	tînt
nous	avons tenu	nous	tinssions
vous	avez tenu	vous	tinssiez
ils	ont tenu	ils	tinssent

CONSTRUCTIONS
tenir à   to be attached to; to care about
tenir à faire   to be keen to do
il ne tient qu'à vous de décider   it's up to you to decide
se tenir   to stand; to take place
être tenu de faire   to be obliged to do

102 tomber

to fall   *also* **retomber**
                        to fall back

PRESENT PARTICIPLE
tombant

PAST PARTICIPLE
tombé

PRESENT

je	**tombe**
tu	**tombes**
il	**tombe**
nous	**tombons**
vous	**tombez**
ils	**tombent**

IMPERFECT

je	**tombais**
tu	**tombais**
il	**tombait**
nous	**tombions**
vous	**tombiez**
ils	**tombaient**

FUTURE

je	**tomberai**
tu	**tomberas**
il	**tombera**
nous	**tomberons**
vous	**tomberez**
ils	**tomberont**

IMPERATIVE

tombe
tombons
tombez

CONDITIONAL

je	**tomberais**
tu	**tomberais**
il	**tomberait**
nous	**tomberions**
vous	**tomberiez**
ils	**tomberaient**

to fall

PAST HISTORIC		PRESENT SUBJUNCTIVE	
je	**tombai**	je	**tombe**
tu	**tombas**	tu	**tombes**
il	**tomba**	il	**tombe**
nous	**tombâmes**	nous	**tombions**
vous	**tombâtes**	vous	**tombiez**
ils	**tombèrent**	ils	**tombent**

PERFECT		PAST SUBJUNCTIVE	
je	**suis tombé**	je	**tombasse**
tu	**es tombé**	tu	**tombasses**
il	**est tombé**	il	**tombât**
nous	**sommes tombés**	nous	**tombassions**
vous	**êtes tombé(s)**	vous	**tombassiez**
ils	**sont tombés**	ils	**tombassent**

CONSTRUCTIONS

tomber de bicyclette/cheval   to fall off one's bicycle/horse
laisser tomber qch   to drop sth
faire tomber   to knock over; to knock down
tomber malade/amoureux   to fall ill/in love
tomber sur   to come across

103 traduire
to translate

PRESENT PARTICIPLE
traduisant

PAST PARTICIPLE
traduit

PRESENT

je	**traduis**
tu	**traduis**
il	**traduit**
nous	**traduisons**
vous	**traduisez**
ils	**traduisent**

IMPERFECT

je	**traduisais**
tu	**traduisais**
il	**traduisait**
nous	**traduisions**
vous	**traduisiez**
ils	**traduisaient**

FUTURE

je	**traduirai**
tu	**traduiras**
il	**traduira**
nous	**traduirons**
vous	**traduirez**
ils	**traduiront**

IMPERATIVE

traduis
traduisons
traduisez

CONDITIONAL

je	**traduirais**
tu	**traduirais**
il	**traduirait**
nous	**traduirions**
vous	**traduiriez**
ils	**traduiraient**

PAST HISTORIC

je	**traduisis**
tu	**traduisis**
il	**traduisit**
nous	**traduisîmes**
vous	**traduisîtes**
ils	**traduisirent**

PRESENT SUBJUNCTIVE

je	**traduise**
tu	**traduises**
il	**traduise**
nous	**traduisions**
vous	**traduisiez**
ils	**traduisent**

PERFECT

j'	**ai traduit**
tu	**as traduit**
il	**a traduit**
nous	**avons traduit**
vous	**avez traduit**
ils	**ont traduit**

PAST SUBJUNCTIVE

je	**traduisisse**
tu	**traduisisses**
il	**traduisît**
nous	**traduisissions**
vous	**traduisissiez**
ils	**traduisissent**

CONSTRUCTIONS
traduit en/du français translated into/from French

104 traire

to milk

PRESENT PARTICIPLE
trayant

PAST PARTICIPLE
trait

also **distraire**
to distract

extraire
to extract

soustraire
to subtract

PRESENT
je	**trais**
tu	**trais**
il	**trait**
nous	**trayons**
vous	**trayez**
ils	**traient**

IMPERFECT
je	**trayais**
tu	**trayais**
il	**trayait**
nous	**trayions**
vous	**trayiez**
ils	**trayaient**

FUTURE
je	**trairai**
tu	**trairas**
il	**traira**
nous	**trairons**
vous	**trairez**
ils	**trairont**

IMPERATIVE
trais
trayons
trayez

CONDITIONAL
je	**trairais**
tu	**trairais**
il	**trairait**
nous	**trairions**
vous	**trairiez**
ils	**trairaient**

PAST HISTORIC	PRESENT SUBJUNCTIVE
not used	je **traie**
	tu **traies**
	il **traie**
	nous **trayions**
	vous **trayiez**
	ils **traient**
PERFECT	PAST SUBJUNCTIVE
j' **ai trait**	*not used*
tu **as trait**	
il **a trait**	
nous **avons trait**	
vous **avez trait**	
ils **ont trait**	

105 vaincre
to defeat   *also* **convaincre**
                                   to convince

PRESENT PARTICIPLE
vainquant

PAST PARTICIPLE
vaincu

PRESENT		*IMPERFECT*	
je	**vaincs**	je	**vainquais**
tu	**vaincs**	tu	**vainquais**
il	**vainc**	il	**vainquait**
nous	**vainquons**	nous	**vainquions**
vous	**vainquez**	vous	**vainquiez**
ils	**vainquent**	ils	**vainquaient**

FUTURE

je	**vaincrai**
tu	**vaincras**
il	**vaincra**
nous	**vaincrons**
vous	**vaincrez**
ils	**vaincront**

IMPERATIVE

vaincs
vainquons
vainquez

CONDITIONAL

je	**vaincrais**
tu	**vaincrais**
il	**vaincrait**
nous	**vaincrions**
vous	**vaincriez**
ils	**vaincraient**

PAST HISTORIC
- je **vainquis**
- tu **vainquis**
- il **vainquit**
- nous **vainquîmes**
- vous **vainquîtes**
- ils **vainquirent**

PERFECT
- j' **ai vaincu**
- tu **as vaincu**
- il **a vaincu**
- nous **avons vaincu**
- vous **avez vaincu**
- ils **ont vaincu**

PRESENT SUBJUNCTIVE
- je **vainque**
- tu **vainques**
- il **vainque**
- nous **vainquions**
- vous **vainquiez**
- ils **vainquent**

PAST SUBJUNCTIVE
- je **vainquisse**
- tu **vainquisses**
- il **vainquît**
- nous **vainquissions**
- vous **vainquissiez**
- ils **vainquissent**

CONSTRUCTIONS
s'avouer vaincu   to admit defeat

106 valoir
to be worth

PRESENT PARTICIPLE
valant

PAST PARTICIPLE
valu

PRESENT
je	**vaux**
tu	**vaux**
il	**vaut**
nous	**val**ons
vous	**val**ez
ils	**val**ent

IMPERFECT
je	**val**ais
tu	**val**ais
il	**val**ait
nous	**val**ions
vous	**val**iez
ils	**val**aient

FUTURE
je	**vaudrai**
tu	**vaudras**
il	**vaudra**
nous	**vaudrons**
vous	**vaudrez**
ils	**vaudront**

IMPERATIVE
vaux
valons
valez

CONDITIONAL
je	**vaudrais**
tu	**vaudrais**
il	**vaudrait**
nous	**vaudrions**
vous	**vaudriez**
ils	**vaudraient**

PAST HISTORIC		PRESENT SUBJUNCTIVE	
je	**valus**	je	**vaille**
tu	**valus**	tu	**vailles**
il	**valut**	il	**vaille**
nous	**valûmes**	nous	**valions**
vous	**valûtes**	vous	**valiez**
ils	**valurent**	ils	**vaillent**

PERFECT		PAST SUBJUNCTIVE	
j'	**ai valu**	je	**valusse**
tu	**as valu**	tu	**valusses**
il	**a valu**	il	**valût**
nous	**avons valu**	nous	**valussions**
vous	**avez valu**	vous	**valussiez**
ils	**ont valu**	ils	**valussent**

CONSTRUCTIONS
valoir cher / 10 F   to be worth a lot / 10 F
cet outil ne vaut rien   this tool is useless
il vaut mieux se taire   it's better to say nothing
ce film vaut la peine d'être vu   this film is worth seeing

107 vendre
to sell

also **défendre**
to defend

PRESENT PARTICIPLE
vendant

dépendre
to depend

PAST PARTICIPLE
vendu

entendre
to hear

PRESENT
je	**vends**
tu	**vends**
il	**vend**
nous	**vendons**
vous	**vendez**
ils	**vendent**

IMPERFECT
je	**vendais**
tu	**vendais**
il	**vendait**
nous	**vendions**
vous	**vendiez**
ils	**vendaient**

FUTURE
je	**vendrai**
tu	**vendras**
il	**vendra**
nous	**vendrons**
vous	**vendrez**
ils	**vendront**

IMPERATIVE

vends
vendons
vendez

CONDITIONAL
je	**vendrais**
tu	**vendrais**
il	**vendrait**
nous	**vendrions**
vous	**vendriez**
ils	**vendraient**

pendre
  to hang

répandre
  to spread

tendre
  to stretch

PAST HISTORIC		PRESENT SUBJUNCTIVE	
je	**vendis**	je	**vende**
tu	**vendis**	tu	**vendes**
il	**vendit**	il	**vende**
nous	**vendîmes**	nous	**vendions**
vous	**vendîtes**	vous	**vendiez**
ils	**vendirent**	ils	**vendent**

PERFECT		PAST SUBJUNCTIVE	
j'	**ai vendu**	je	**vendisse**
tu	**as vendu**	tu	**vendisses**
il	**a vendu**	il	**vendît**
nous	**avons vendu**	nous	**vendissions**
vous	**avez vendu**	vous	**vendissiez**
ils	**ont vendu**	ils	**vendissent**

CONSTRUCTIONS

vendre qch à qn to sell sb sth
il me l'a vendu 10 F he sold it to me for 10 F
'à vendre' 'for sale'
ils se vendent à la pièce / douzaine they are sold
singly / by the dozen

108 venir

to come   *also*   **intervenir**
                 to intervene

PRESENT PARTICIPLE
  venant   **parvenir**
                    to succeed

PAST PARTICIPLE
  venu   **survenir**
                    to occur

PRESENT		*IMPERFECT*	
je	viens	je	**ven**ais
tu	viens	tu	**ven**ais
il	vient	il	**ven**ait
nous	**ven**ons	nous	**ven**ions
vous	**ven**ez	vous	**ven**iez
ils	viennent	ils	**ven**aient

		FUTURE	
		je	viendrai
		tu	viendras
		il	viendra
		nous	viendrons
		vous	viendrez
		ils	viendront

IMPERATIVE		*CONDITIONAL*	
	viens	je	viendrais
	venons	tu	viendrais
	venez	il	viendrait
		nous	viendrions
		vous	viendriez
		ils	viendraient

to come

PAST HISTORIC		PRESENT SUBJUNCTIVE	
je	vins	je	vienne
tu	vins	tu	viennes
il	vint	il	vienne
nous	vînmes	nous	venions
vous	vîntes	vous	veniez
ils	vinrent	ils	viennent

PERFECT		PAST SUBJUNCTIVE	
je	suis venu	je	vinsse
tu	es venu	tu	vinsses
il	est venu	il	vînt
nous	sommes venus	nous	vinssions
vous	êtes venu(s)	vous	vinssiez
ils	sont venus	ils	vinssent

CONSTRUCTIONS
venir de Paris to come from Paris
faire venir qn to call *or* send for sb
venir de faire qch to have just done sth
en venir à faire qch to be reduced to doing sth

109 vêtir

to dress   *also* **revêtir**

            to put on

PRESENT PARTICIPLE
vêtant

PAST PARTICIPLE
vêtu

PRESENT
je	vêts
tu	vêts
il	vêt
nous	vêtons
vous	vêtez
ils	vêtent

IMPERFECT
je	vêtais
tu	vêtais
il	vêtait
nous	vêtions
vous	vêtiez
ils	vêtaient

FUTURE
je	vêtirai
tu	vêtiras
il	vêtira
nous	vêtirons
vous	vêtirez
ils	vêtiront

IMPERATIVE

         vêts
         vêtons
         vêtez

CONDITIONAL
je	vêtirais
tu	vêtirais
il	vêtirait
nous	vêtirions
vous	vêtiriez
ils	vêtiraient

PAST HISTORIC

je	vêtis
tu	vêtis
il	vêtit
nous	vêtîmes
vous	vêtîtes
ils	vêtirent

PERFECT

j'	ai vêtu
tu	as vêtu
il	a vêtu
nous	avons vêtu
vous	avez vêtu
ils	ont vêtu

PRESENT SUBJUNCTIVE

je	vête
tu	vêtes
il	vête
nous	vêtions
vous	vêtiez
ils	vêtent

PAST SUBJUNCTIVE

je	vêtisse
tu	vêtisses
il	vêtît
nous	vêtissions
vous	vêtissiez
ils	vêtissent

CONSTRUCTIONS

vêtu d'un pantalon et d'un chandail   wearing trousers
and a sweater
se vêtir   to dress

110 vivre
to live

also **survivre**
to survive

PRESENT PARTICIPLE
vivant

PAST PARTICIPLE
vécu

PRESENT
je	**vis**
tu	**vis**
il	**vit**
nous	**vivons**
vous	**vivez**
ils	**vivent**

IMPERFECT
je	**vivais**
tu	**vivais**
il	**vivait**
nous	**vivions**
vous	**viviez**
ils	**vivaient**

FUTURE
je	**vivrai**
tu	**vivras**
il	**vivra**
nous	**vivrons**
vous	**vivrez**
ils	**vivront**

IMPERATIVE
vis
vivons
vivez

CONDITIONAL
je	**vivrais**
tu	**vivrais**
il	**vivrait**
nous	**vivrions**
vous	**vivriez**
ils	**vivraient**

PAST HISTORIC		PRESENT SUBJUNCTIVE	
je	vécus	je	vive
tu	vécus	tu	vives
il	vécut	il	vive
nous	vécûmes	nous	vivions
vous	vécûtes	vous	viviez
ils	vécurent	ils	vivent

PERFECT		PAST SUBJUNCTIVE	
j'	ai vécu	je	vécusse
tu	as vécu	tu	vécusses
il	a vécu	il	vécût
nous	avons vécu	nous	vécussions
vous	avez vécu	vous	vécussiez
ils	ont vécu	ils	vécussent

CONSTRUCTIONS

il vit à la campagne/en France he lives in the country/in France

vivre de rentes/légumes to live on a private income/on vegetables

il est facile/difficile à vivre he's easy/difficult to get on with

111 voir

to see

also **entrevoir**
to catch a glimpse of

PRESENT PARTICIPLE
voyant

revoir
to revise

PAST PARTICIPLE
vu

PRESENT
je	**vois**
tu	**vois**
il	**voit**
nous	**voyons**
vous	**voyez**
ils	**voient**

IMPERFECT
je	**voyais**
tu	**voyais**
il	**voyait**
nous	**voyions**
vous	**voyiez**
ils	**voyaient**

FUTURE
je	**verrai**
tu	**verras**
il	**verra**
nous	**verrons**
vous	**verrez**
ils	**verront**

IMPERATIVE
vois
voyons
voyez

CONDITIONAL
je	**verrais**
tu	**verrais**
il	**verrait**
nous	**verrions**
vous	**verriez**
ils	**verraient**

to see

PAST HISTORIC		PRESENT SUBJUNCTIVE	
je	vis	je	voie
tu	vis	tu	voies
il	vit	il	voie
nous	vîmes	nous	voyions
vous	vîtes	vous	voyiez
ils	virent	ils	voient

PERFECT		PAST SUBJUNCTIVE	
j'	ai vu	je	visse
tu	as vu	tu	visses
il	a vu	il	vît
nous	avons vu	nous	vissions
vous	avez vu	vous	vissiez
ils	ont vu	ils	vissent

CONSTRUCTIONS

aller voir qn to go and see sb
faire voir qch to show sth
on verra bien we'll soon see
ça n'a rien à voir avec notre problème it's got nothing to do with our problem
voyons! come now!

112 vouloir
to want

PRESENT PARTICIPLE
voulant

PAST PARTICIPLE
voulu

PRESENT
je	**veux**
tu	**veux**
il	**veut**
nous	**voulons**
vous	**voulez**
ils	**veulent**

IMPERFECT
je	**voulais**
tu	**voulais**
il	**voulait**
nous	**voulions**
vous	**vouliez**
ils	**voulaient**

FUTURE
je	**voudrai**
tu	**voudras**
il	**voudra**
nous	**voudrons**
vous	**voudrez**
ils	**voudront**

IMPERATIVE
veuille
veuillons
veuillez

CONDITIONAL
je	**voudrais**
tu	**voudrais**
il	**voudrait**
nous	**voudrions**
vous	**voudriez**
ils	**voudraient**

to want

<table>
<tr><td colspan="2">PAST HISTORIC</td><td colspan="2">PRESENT SUBJUNCTIVE</td></tr>
<tr><td>je</td><td>voulus</td><td>je</td><td>veuille</td></tr>
<tr><td>tu</td><td>voulus</td><td>tu</td><td>veuilles</td></tr>
<tr><td>il</td><td>voulut</td><td>il</td><td>veuille</td></tr>
<tr><td>nous</td><td>voulûmes</td><td>nous</td><td>voulions</td></tr>
<tr><td>vous</td><td>voulûtes</td><td>vous</td><td>vouliez</td></tr>
<tr><td>ils</td><td>voulurent</td><td>ils</td><td>veuillent</td></tr>
<tr><td colspan="2">PERFECT</td><td colspan="2">PAST SUBJUNCTIVE</td></tr>
<tr><td>j'</td><td>ai voulu</td><td>je</td><td>voulusse</td></tr>
<tr><td>tu</td><td>as voulu</td><td>tu</td><td>voulusses</td></tr>
<tr><td>il</td><td>a voulu</td><td>il</td><td>voulût</td></tr>
<tr><td>nous</td><td>avons voulu</td><td>nous</td><td>voulussions</td></tr>
<tr><td>vous</td><td>avez voulu</td><td>vous</td><td>voulussiez</td></tr>
<tr><td>ils</td><td>ont voulu</td><td>ils</td><td>voulussent</td></tr>
</table>

CONSTRUCTIONS

vouloir faire qch   to want to do sth
je veux bien le faire   I'm happy to do it; I don't mind doing it
en vouloir à qn   to have something against sb
vouloir dire   to mean

INDEX

(a) Each verb is numerically cross-referred to one of the 112 verb models shown in colour. Defective verbs, however, are cross-referred to page 13.
(b) All entries are arranged in alphabetical order; for alphabetisation purposes, pronouns are not included: s'asseoir, se taire etc appear as asseoir (s'), taire (se) etc.
(c) With the exception of those verbs which are individually marked (see note (d)), and of Reflexive and Reciprocal verbs which are always conjugated with être, a verb's auxiliary is that of its verb model.
(d) Superior numbers refer you to notes on page 256, which outline how the verb deviates from its verb model.
(e) An asterisk (★) indicates that the verb is conjugated with être when intransitive and avoir when transitive.

abaisser	36	accuser	36	aider	36
abandonner	36	acharner (s')	36	aigrir	45
abattre	11	acheminer	36	aiguiser	36
abêtir	45	**acheter**	1	aimanter	36
abîmer	36	achever	52	aimer	36
abolir	45	**acquérir**	2	ajouter	36
abonder	36	actionner	36	ajuster	36
abonner	36	activer	36	alarmer	36
aborder	36	adapter	36	alerter	36
aboutir	45	additionner	36	alimenter	36
aboyer	63	adhérer	41	allécher	41
abréger	80	adjoindre	51	alléger	80
abreuver	36	admettre	56	alléguer	41
abriter	36	admirer	36	**aller**	3
abrutir	45	adopter	36	allier	25
absenter (s')	36	adorer	36	allumer	36
absorber	36	adosser	36	altérer	41
absoudre[4]	85	adoucir	45	alterner	36
abstenir (s')	101	adresser	36	alunir	45
abstraire	104	advenir[3]	108	amaigrir	45
abuser	36	aérer	41	ambitionner	36
accabler	36	affaiblir	45	améliorer	36
accaparer	36	affairer (s')	36	aménager	54
accéder	41	affaisser (s')	36	amener	52
accélérer	41	affamer	36	ameuter	36
accepter	36	affermir	45	amincir	45
accompagner	36	afficher	36	amoindrir	45
accomplir	45	affirmer	36	amollir	45
accorder	36	affliger	54	amonceler	4
accoter	36	affoler	36	amorcer	15
accoucher	36	affranchir	45	amplifier	25
accouder (s')	36	affréter	41	amputer	36
accourir[5]	21	affronter	36	amuser	36
accoutumer	36	agacer	15	analyser	36
accrocher	36	agenouiller (s')	36	anéantir	45
accroire	*page 13*	agir	45	angoisser	36
accroître[6]	27	agiter	36	animer	36
accroupir (s')	45	agrandir	45	annexer	36
accueillir	28	agréer	24	annoncer	15
accumuler	36	ahurir	45	annoter	36

annuler	36	assagir	45	avancer	15
anoblir	45	**assaillir**	7	avantager	54
anticiper	36	assainir	45	aventurer	36
apaiser	36	assassiner	36	avertir	45
apercevoir	81	assembler	36	aveugler	36
apitoyer	63	assener	52	avilir	45
aplatir	45	**asseoir (s')**	8	aviser	36
apparaître[2]	67	asservir	45	aviver	36
appareiller	36	assiéger	80	**avoir**	10
apparenter	36	assigner	36	avouer	36
apparier	25	assimiler	36	bâcler	36
apparoir	*page 13*	assister	36	bafouer	36
appartenir	101	associer	25	bagarrer (se)	36
appauvrir	45	assombrir	45	baigner	36
appeler	4	assommer	36	bâiller	36
applaudir	45	assortir	45	baiser	36
appliquer	36	assoupir	45	baisser	36
apporter	36	assouplir	45	balader (se)	36
apprécier	25	assourdir	45	balafrer	36
apprendre	5	assujettir	45	balancer	15
apprêter	36	assumer	36	balayer	70
apprivoiser	36	assurer	36	balbutier	25
approcher	36	astiquer	36	baliser	36
approfondir	45	astreindre	71	bannir	45
approprier	25	atermoyer	63	baptiser	36
approuver	36	attabler (s')	36	baratiner	36
appuyer	63	attacher	36	barbouiller	36
arc-bouter	36	attaquer	36	barioler	36
argenter	36	atteindre	71	barrer	36
arguer	36	atteler	4	barricader	36
armer	36	**attendre**	9	basculer	36
arpenter	36	attendrir	45	baser	36
arracher	36	atterrir	45	batailler	36
arranger	54	attirer	36	batifoler	36
arrêter	36	attraper	36	bâtir	45
arriver	6	attribuer	36	**battre**	11
arrondir	45	augmenter	36	bavarder	36
arroser	36	autoriser	36	baver	36
asphyxier	25	avachir (s')	45	bêcher	36
aspirer	36	avaler	36	becqueter	50

240

béer	*page 13*	bousiller	36	capturer	36
bégayer	70	boutonner	36	caractériser	36
bêler	36	braconner	36	caresser	36
bénéficier	25	brailler	36	caricaturer	36
bénir	45	braire[7]	104	caser	36
bercer	15	brancher	36	casser	36
berner	36	brandir	45	cataloguer	36
beugler	36	branler	36	catapulter	36
beurrer	36	braquer	36	causer	36
biaiser	36	braver	36	céder	41
bichonner	36	bredouiller	36	ceindre	71
biffer	36	breveter	30	célébrer	41
blaguer	36	bricoler	36	celer	1
blâmer	36	brider	36	celer	36
blanchir	45	briguer	36	cercler	36
blaser	36	briller	36	certifier	25
blêmir	45	brimer	36	cesser	36
blesser	36	briser	36	chagriner	36
bloquer	36	broder	36	chahuter	36
blottir (se)	45	broncher	36	chamailler	36
boire	12	brosser	36	chanceler	4
boiter	36	brouiller	36	changer	54
bombarder	36	broyer	63	chanter	36
bondir	45	brûler	36	chantonner	36
bonifier	25	brunir	45	charger	54
border	36	buter	36	charmer	36
borner	36	cabrer (se)	36	charrier	25
boucher	36	cacher	36	chasser	36
boucler	36	cadrer	36	châtier	25
bouder	36	cajoler	36	chatouiller	36
bouffer	36	calculer	36	chauffer	36
bouffir	45	caler	36	chausser	36
bouger	54	câliner	36	chercher	36
bouillir	13	calmer	36	chérir	45
bouleverser	36	calomnier	25	chiffrer	36
boulonner	36	calquer	36	choir	*page 13*
bourdonner	36	camper	36	choisir	45
bourrer	36	capituler	36	chômer	36
boursoufler	36	capter	36	choquer	36
bousculer	36	captiver	36	choyer	63

couvrir	22	déboutonner	36	décourager	54
cracher	36	débrailler (se)	36	**découvrir**	**30**
craindre	23	débrancher	36	décréter	41
craquer	36	débrayer	70	décrier	25
créer	24	débrouiller	36	décrire	38
crépir	45	débuter	36	décrocher	36
creuser	36	décaler	36	décroître[10]	27
crever	52	décanter	36	dédaigner	36
cribler	36	décaper	36	dédicacer	15
crier	25	décapoter	36	dédier	25
critiquer	36	décéder[2]	41	dédire	48
crocheter	1	déceler	1	dédommager	54
croire	26	décélérer	41	dédouaner	36
croiser	36	décentraliser	36	dédoubler	36
croître	27	décerner	36	déduire	29
crouler	36	décevoir	81	défaillir[11]	7
croupir	45	déchaîner	36	défaire	43
crucifier	25	décharger	54	défalquer	36
cueillir	28	déchiffrer	36	défavoriser	36
cuire	29	déchiqueter	50	défendre	107
culbuter	36	déchirer	36	déférer	41
cultiver	36	déchoir *page 13*		déficeler	4
cumuler	36	décider	36	défier	25
curer	36	décimer	36	défigurer	36
daigner	36	déclamer	36	défiler	36
damner	36	déclarer	36	définir	45
danser	36	déclasser	36	défoncer	15
dater	36	déclencher	36	déformer	36
débarquer	36	décliner	36	défraîchir	45
débarrasser	36	décoder	36	dégager	54
débattre	11	décolérer	41	dégainer	36
débaucher	36	décoller	36	dégauchir	45
débiliter	36	décommander	36	dégazonner	36
débiter	36	déconcerter	36	dégeler	1
déblatérer	41	déconseiller	36	dégénérer	41
débloquer	36	décontracter	36	dégonfler	36
déboîter	36	décorer	36	dégourdir	45
déborder	36	découdre	20	dégoûter	36
déboucher	36	découler	36	dégrader	36
débourser	36	découper	36	dégringoler	36

dégriser	36	départager	54	désennuyer	63
déguerpir	45	départir (se)	68	désensibiliser	36
déguiser	36	dépasser	69	désentraver	36
déguster	36	dépayser	36	déséquilibrer	36
déjeter	50	dépecer	52	déserter	36
déjeuner	36	dépêcher	36	désespérer	41
déjouer	36	dépeindre	71	déshabiller	36
délaisser	36	dépendre	107	déshabituer	36
délayer	70	dépenser	36	déshériter	36
déléguer	41	dépérir	45	désigner	36
délibérer	41	dépister	36	désinfecter	36
délier	25	déplacer	15	désintégrer	41
délirer	36	déplaire	74	désintéresser	36
délivrer	36	déplier	25	désintoxiquer	36
déloger	54	déployer	63	désirer	36
demander	36	dépolir	45	désister (se)	36
démanteler	1	déposer	36	désobéir	45
démarquer	36	dépouiller	36	désoler	36
démarrer	36	dépoussiérer	41	désorganiser	36
démêler	36	déprécier	25	désorienter	36
déménager	54	déprendre	78	dessaisir	45
démener (se)	52	déprimer	36	dessécher	41
démentir	92	déraciner	36	desserrer	36
démettre	56	déranger	54	dessiner	36
demeurer[12]	36	déraper	36	destiner	36
démissionner	36	dérégler	41	destituer	36
démolir	45	déroger	54	désunir	45
démonter[1]	57	dérouler	36	détacher	36
démontrer	36	dérouter	36	détailler	36
démultiplier	25	désaccoutumer	36	détecter	36
démunir	45	désagréger	80	déteindre	71
dénaturer	36	désaltérer	41	dételer	4
dénier	25	désamorcer	15	détendre	107
dénigrer	36	désapprendre	5	détenir	101
déniveler	4	désapprouver	36	détériorer	36
dénombrer	36	désassortir	45	déterminer	36
dénoncer	15	désavantager	54	détester	36
dénouer	36	désavouer	36	détordre	58
dépanner	36	descendre*	31	détourner	36
dépaqueter	50	désemparer	36	détraquer	36

émouvoir[15]	61	enjoliver	36	épater	36
emparer (s')	36	enlacer	15	épeler	4
empêcher	36	enlever	52	éplucher	36
empiéter	41	enneiger	54	éponger	94
empirer	36	ennuyer	63	épouser	36
emplir	45	énoncer	15	épouvanter	36
employer	63	enquérir (s')	2	épreindre	71
empoisonner	36	enquêter	36	éprendre (s')	78
emporter	36	enraciner	36	éprouver	36
emprisonner	36	enrager	54	épuiser	36
emprunter	36	enregistrer	36	équilibrer	36
encadrer	36	enrichir	45	équiper	36
encaisser	36	enrouler	36	équivaloir	106
enchaîner	36	enseigner	36	esclaffer (s')	36
enchanter	36	ensevelir	45	escorter	36
encombrer	36	ensuivre (s')[3]	98	**espérer**	**41**
encourager	54	entamer	36	esquisser	36
encourir	21	entasser	36	esquiver	36
endetter	36	entendre	107	essayer	70
endoctriner	36	enterrer	36	essorer	36
endommager	54	enthousiasmer	36	essouffler	36
endormir (s')	37	entourer	36	essuyer	63
enduire	29	entraîner	36	estimer	36
endurcir	45	entraver	36	estropier	25
énerver	36	entrelacer	15	établir	45
enfanter	36	entremettre (s')	56	étaler	36
enfermer	36	entreprendre	78	étayer	70
enfiler	36	**entrer**★	**39**	éteindre	71
enflammer	36	entretenir	101	étendre	107
enfler	36	entrevoir	111	éternuer	36
enfoncer	15	énumérer	41	étiqueter	50
enfouir	45	envahir	45	étirer	36
enfreindre	71	envelopper	36	étoffer	36
enfuir (s')	46	envisager	54	étonner	36
engager	54	envoler (s')	36	étouffer	36
engloutir	45	**envoyer**	**40**	étourdir	45
engourdir	45	épandre	107	étrangler	36
engraisser	36	épanouir	45	**être**	**42**
engueuler	36	épargner	36	étreindre	71
enivrer	36	éparpiller	36	étudier	25

évader (s')	36	exterminer	36	flairer	36
évaluer	36	extraire	104	flamber	36
évanouir (s')	45	exulter	36	flâner	36
évaporer	36	fabriquer	36	flanquer	36
éveiller	36	fâcher	36	flatter	36
éventer	36	faciliter	36	fléchir	45
évertuer (s')	36	façonner	36	flétrir	45
éviter	36	facturer	36	fleurir[16]	45
évoluer	36	faillir	*page 13*	flotter	36
évoquer	36	**faire**	43	foisonner	36
exagérer	41	**falloir**	44	fomenter	36
exalter	36	falsifier	25	foncer	15
examiner	36	familiariser	36	fonctionner	36
exaspérer	41	farcir	45	fonder	36
excéder	41	fasciner	36	fondre	84
excepter	36	fatiguer	36	forcer	15
exciter	36	faucher	36	forger	54
exclamer (s')	36	faufiler	36	formaliser (se)	36
exclure	17	fausser	36	former	36
excommunier	25	favoriser	36	formuler	36
excuser	36	feindre	71	fortifier	25
exécrer	41	feinter	36	foudroyer	63
exécuter	36	fêler	36	fouetter	36
exempter	36	féliciter	36	fouiller	36
exhiber	36	fendre	107	fourmiller	36
exhorter	36	ferler	36	fournir	45
exiger	54	fermenter	36	fourrer	36
exiler	36	fermer	36	fourvoyer	63
exister	36	fêter	36	fracasser	36
exonérer	41	feuilleter	50	franchir	45
expédier	25	fiancer	15	frapper	36
expérimenter	36	ficeler	4	frayer	70
expirer	36	ficher	36	freiner	36
expliquer	36	fier	25	frémir	45
exploiter	36	figer	54	fréquenter	36
exploser	36	filer	36	frire[17]	97
exporter	36	fileter	1	friser	36
exposer	36	financer	15	frissonner	36
exprimer	36	**finir**	45	froisser	36
expulser	36	fixer	36	frôler	36

froncer	15	gravir	45	heurter	36
frotter	36	greffer	36	hocher	36
frustrer	36	grêler	36	honorer	36
fuir	**46**	griffonner	36	horrifier	25
fumer	36	grignoter	36	huer	36
fusiller	36	griller	36	humaniser	36
gâcher	36	grimacer	15	humidifier	25
gagner	36	grimper	36	humilier	25
galoper	36	grincer	15	hurler	36
garantir	45	griser	36	hypnotiser	36
garder	36	grogner	36	idéaliser	36
garer	36	grommeler	4	identifier	25
garnir	45	gronder	36	ignorer	36
gaspiller	36	grossir	45	illuminer	36
gâter	36	grouiller	36	illustrer	36
gauchir	45	grouper	36	imaginer	36
gaufrer	36	guérir	45	imiter	36
gausser (se)	36	guerroyer	63	immigrer	36
geindre	71	guetter	36	immiscer (s')	15
geler	1	guider	36	immobiliser	36
gémir	45	guinder	36	immoler	36
gêner	36	habiller	36	impatienter	36
généraliser	36	habiter	36	impliquer	36
gérer	41	habituer	36	implorer	36
gésir	*page 13*	hacher	36	importer	36
giboyer	63	**haïr**	**47**	impressionner	36
gifler	36	haleter	1	imprimer	36
givrer	36	handicaper	36	improviser	36
glacer	15	hanter	36	inaugurer	36
glisser	36	harceler	4	inciter	36
glorifier	25	harmoniser	36	incliner	36
gommer	36	hasarder	36	inclure[18]	17
gonfler	36	hâter	36	incommoder	36
goûter	36	hausser	36	incorporer	36
gouverner	36	héberger	54	incriminer	36
gracier	25	hébéter	41	inculper	36
grandir	45	hennir	45	indiquer	36
gratifier	25	hérisser	36	induire	29
gratter	36	hériter	36	infecter	36
graver	36	hésiter	36	infester	36

infirmer	36	invoquer	36	lorgner	36
infliger	54	irriter	36	lotir	45
influencer	15	isoler	36	loucher	36
informer	36	jaillir	45	louer	36
ingénier (s')	25	jaser	36	louper	36
inhaler	36	jaunir	45	louvoyer	63
initier	25	**jeter**	**50**	lubrifier	25
injurier	25	jeûner	36	lutter	36
innover	36	**joindre**	**51**	mâcher	36
inoculer	36	jouer	36	machiner	36
inonder	36	jouir	45	magnifier	25
inquiéter	41	juger	54	maigrir	45
inscrire	38	jumeler	4	maintenir	101
insensibiliser	36	jurer	36	maîtriser	36
insérer	41	justifier	25	majorer	36
insinuer	36	labourer	36	malfaire	43
insister	36	lacer	15	malmener	52
inspecter	36	lâcher	36	maltraiter	36
inspirer	36	laisser	36	**manger**	**54**
installer	36	lamenter (se)	36	manier	25
instituer	36	lancer	15	manifester	36
instruire	29	languir	45	manigancer	15
insulter	36	larmoyer	63	manipuler	36
insurger (s')	54	laver	36	manœuvrer	36
intégrer	41	lécher	41	manquer	36
intensifier	25	légaliser	36	manufacturer	36
intercéder	41	légiférer	41	manutentionner	36
interdire	**48**	lésiner	36	marcher	36
intéresser	36	**lever**	**52**	marier	25
interloquer	36	libérer	41	marquer	36
interroger	54	licencier	25	marteler	1
interrompre	90	lier	25	masquer	36
intervenir	108	ligoter	36	massacrer	36
intituler	36	limer	36	masser	36
intriguer	36	limiter	36	matérialiser	36
introduire	**49**	liquéfier	25	**maudire**	**55**
inventer	36	liquider	36	maugréer	24
invertir	45	**lire**	**53**	mécaniser	36
investir	45	livrer	36	méconnaître	19
inviter	36	loger	54	mécontenter	36

médire	48	mortifier	25	obliger	54
méditer	36	motiver	36	oblitérer	41
méfaire	43	moucher	36	obscurcir	45
méfier (se)	25	**moudre**	**59**	obséder	41
mélanger	54	mouiller	36	observer	36
mêler	36	**mourir**	**60**	obstiner (s')	36
menacer	15	**mouvoir**	**61**	**obtenir**	**64**
ménager	54	muer	36	occuper	36
mendier	25	multiplier	25	octroyer	63
mener	52	munir	45	offenser	36
mentionner	36	mûrir	45	**offrir**	**65**
mentir	92	murmurer	36	oindre *page 13*	
méprendre (se)	78	museler	4	omettre	56
mépriser	36	muter	36	opérer	41
mériter	36	mutiler	36	opposer	36
messeoir *page 13*		mystifier	25	opprimer	36
mesurer	36	nager	54	ordonner	36
mettre	**56**	**naître**	**62**	organiser	36
meubler	36	nantir	45	orner	36
meugler	36	narrer	36	orthographier	25
meurtrir	45	naviguer	36	osciller	36
miauler	36	navrer	36	oser	36
mijoter	36	nécessiter	36	ôter	36
mimer	36	négliger	54	oublier	25
miner	36	négocier	25	ouïr *page 13*	
minimiser	36	neiger	54	outrager	54
mobiliser	36	**nettoyer**	**63**	**ouvrir**	**66**
modeler	1	nier	25	oxyder	36
modérer	41	niveler	4	pacifier	25
moderniser	36	noircir	45	paître *page 13*	
modifier	25	nommer	36	pâlir	45
moisir	45	normaliser	36	palper	36
moissonner	36	noter	36	palpiter	36
mollir	45	nouer	36	panser	36
monnayer	70	nourrir	45	parachever	52
monopoliser	36	noyer	63	parachuter	36
monter★	**57**	nuire[19]	29	**paraître**	**67**
montrer	36	numéroter	36	paralyser	36
moquer (se)	36	obéir	45	parcourir	21
mordre	**58**	objecter	36	pardonner	36

punir	45	rassembler	36	recueillir	28
purifier	25	rasséréner	41	recuire	29
qualifier	25	rassurer	36	reculer	36
quereller	36	rater	36	récupérer	41
questionner	36	rationaliser	36	recycler	36
quêter	36	rattraper	36	redescendre	31
quitter	36	ravir	45	rédiger	54
rabattre	11	ravitailler	36	redire	35
raccommoder	36	réagir	45	redoubler	36
raccompagner	36	réaliser	36	redouter	36
raccorder	36	rebattre	11	redresser	36
raccourcir	45	rebondir	45	réduire	29
raccrocher	36	rebuter	36	refaire	43
racheter	1	receler	1	référer	41
racler	36	recenser	36	refermer	36
racoler	36	**recevoir**	81	réfléchir	45
raconter	36	réchapper	36	refléter	41
raffermir	45	réchauffer	36	refondre	84
raffiner	36	rechercher	36	réformer	36
râfler	36	réciter	36	refroidir	45
rafraîchir	45	réclamer	36	réfugier (se)	25
ragaillardir	45	récolter	36	refuser	36
raidir	45	recommander	36	réfuter	36
railler	36	recommencer	15	regagner	36
raisonner	36	récompenser	36	regaillardir	45
rajeunir	45	réconcilier	25	regarder	36
rajouter	36	reconduire	18	régénérer	41
rajuster	36	réconforter	36	régir	45
ralentir	45	reconnaître	19	régler	41
rallier	25	reconquérir	2	régner	41
rallonger	94	reconstruire	29	regretter	36
rallumer	36	reconvertir	45	regrouper	36
ramasser	36	recopier	25	réhabiliter	36
ramener	52	recoudre	20	réhabituer	36
ramollir	45	recourir	21	rehausser	36
ranimer	36	recouvrir	22	réimprimer	36
rappeler	4	récréer	24	réintégrer	41
rapporter	36	récrier (se)	25	rejaillir	45
rapprocher	36	récrire	38	rejeter	50
raser	36	rectifier	25	rejoindre	51

253

tolérer	41	tricher	36	verdoyer	63
tomber	102	tricoter	36	vérifier	25
tondre	84	trier	25	vernir	45
tonner	36	triompher	36	verrouiller	36
tordre	58	tripoter	36	verser	36
torpiller	36	tromper	36	**vêtir**	109
tortiller	36	troquer	36	vexer	36
torturer	36	trotter	36	vibrer	36
toucher	36	troubler	36	vider	36
tourmenter	36	trouer	36	vieillir	45
tourner	36	trouver	36	violer	36
tournoyer	63	truffer	36	virer	36
tousser	36	truquer	36	viser	36
tracasser	36	tuer	36	visiter	36
tracer	15	tutoyer	63	visser	36
traduire	103	ulcérer	41	vitrifier	25
trahir	45	unifier	25	vitupérer	41
traîner	36	unir	45	vivifier	25
traire	104	urbaniser	36	**vivre**	110
traiter	36	user	36	vociférer	41
transcrire	38	usiner	36	voiler	36
transférer	41	utiliser	36	**voir**	111
transformer	36	vacciner	36	voler	36
transmettre	56	**vaincre**	105	vomir	45
transparaître	67	**valoir**	106	voter	36
transpirer	36	vanter	36	vouer	36
transplanter	36	varier	25	**vouloir**	112
transporter	36	végéter	41	vouvoyer	63
traquer	36	veiller	36	voyager	54
travailler	36	vendanger	54	vrombir	45
traverser	36	**vendre**	107	vulgariser	36
trébucher	36	venger	54	zébrer	41
trembler	36	**venir**	108	zézayer	70
tremper	36	verdir	45	zigzaguer	36

NOTES

1) *Auxiliary* = avoir.
2) *Auxiliary* = être.
3) *Only infinitive and 3rd persons of each tense used.*
4) *Past participle:* absous, absoute; *Past Historic and Past Subjunctive not used.*
5) *Conjugated with either* avoir *or* être.
6) *No circumflex on:* j'accrois, tu accrois, j'accrus, tu accrus, il accrut, ils accrurent, j'accrusse *etc,* accru.
7) *Hardly used except in infinitive and 3rd persons of Present, Future and Conditional.*
8) *Past participle:* circoncis.
9) *Past participle:* confit.
10) *As for* (6).
11) *Present tense singular, Future and Conditional tenses least common.*
12) *'To live': auxiliary* = avoir; *'to remain': auxiliary* = être.
13) *Past participle:* dissous, dissoute; *Past Historic and Past Subjunctive not used.*
14) *Auxiliary* = être; *NB:* il éclot; *hardly used except in 3rd persons.*
15) *Past participle:* ému.
16) *'To prosper': present participle* = florissant; *Imperfect* = florissait.
17) *Past participle:* frit; *used mainly in singular of Present tense and in compound tenses.*
18) *Past participle:* inclus.
19) *Past participle:* nui.
20) *In interrogative form,* 'puis' *is substituted for* 'peux': puis-je vous aider? = *may I help you?*
21) *Present Subjunctive:* je prévale *etc.*
22) *Future:* je prévoirai *etc; Conditional:* je prévoirais *etc.*
23) *Past participle:* promu; *used only in infinitive, both participles, and compound tenses.*
24) *Past participle:* relui; *Past Historic:* je reluis *etc.*
25) *No past participle – no compound tenses.*